S0-DMG-751

POOR and MINORITY HEALTH CARE

Gary E. McCuen

IDEAS IN CONFLICT SERIES

publications inc.

411 Mallalieu Drive
Hudson, Wisconsin 54016

ST. PHILIP'S COLLEGE LIBRARY

All rights reserved. No part of this book may be reproduced or stored by any means without prior permission from the copyright owner.

Illustrations & Photo Credits
H. Clay Bennett 93, Bureau of the Census 12, German Democratic Republic Ministry of Health 172, Guardian 105, Herblock 119, Don Hesse 111, Craig MacIntosh 187, Bill Sanders 42, 161, David Seavey 25, 49, 143, Carol & Simpson 41, Swedish Institute 177, John Trever 33, U.S. Department of Health Education and Welfare 16, 59, 67, 75, 86, Fred Wright 135, Richard Wright 99

© 1988 by Gary E. McCuen Publications, Inc.
411 Mallalieu Drive ● Hudson, Wisconsin 54016
(715) 386-5662
Library of Congress Catalog Card
Number: 87-91953

International Standard Book Number 0-86596-065-8
publications inc. Printed in the United States of America

CONTENTS

ST. PHILIP'S COLLEGE LIBRARY.

CHAPTER 3 HEALTH CARE ALTERNATIVES FOR THE POOR

CHAPTER 4 PRIVATIZING HEALTH CARE FOR THE POOR

CHAPTER 5   HEALTH CARE SYSTEMS:
A GLOBAL PERSPECTIVE

REASONING SKILL DEVELOPMENT

These activities may be used as individualized study guides for students in libraries and resource centers or as discussion catalysts in small group and classroom discussions.

IDEAS in CONFLICT ®

This series features ideas in conflict on political, social and moral issues. It presents counterpoints, debates, opinions, commentary and analysis for use in libraries and classrooms. Each title in the series uses one or more of the following basic elements:

Introductions that present an issue overview giving historic background and/or a description of the controversy.

Counterpoints and debates carefully chosen from publications, books, and position papers on the political right and left to help librarians and teachers respond to requests that treatment of public issues be fair and balanced.

Symposiums and forums that go beyond debates that can polarize and oversimplify. These present commentary from across the political spectrum that reflect how complex issues attract many shades of opinion.

A global emphasis with foreign perspectives and surveys on various moral questions and political issues that will help readers to place subject matter in a less culture-bound and ethno-centric frame of reference. In an ever shrinking and interdependent world, understanding and cooperation are essential. Many issues are global in nature and can be effectively dealt with only by common efforts and international understanding.

Reasoning skill study guides and discussion activities provide ready made tools for helping with critical reading and evaluation of content. The guides and activities deal with one or more of the following:

RECOGNIZING AUTHOR'S POINT OF VIEW

INTERPRETING EDITORIAL CARTOONS

VALUES IN CONFLICT

WHAT IS EDITORIAL BIAS?

WHAT IS SEX BIAS?
WHAT IS POLITICAL BIAS?
WHAT IS ETHNOCENTRIC BIAS?
WHAT IS RACE BIAS?
WHAT IS RELIGIOUS BIAS?

*From across **the political spectrum** varied sources are presented for research projects and classroom discussions. Diverse opinions in the series come from magazines, newspapers, syndicated columnists, books, political speeches, foreign nations, and position papers by corporations and non-profit institutions.*

About the Editor

Gary E. McCuen is an editor and publisher of anthologies for public libraries and curriculum materials for schools. Over the past 17 years his publications of over 200 titles have specialized in social, moral and political conflict. They include books, pamphlets, cassettes, tabloids, filmstrips and simulation games, many of them designed from his curriculums during 11 years of teaching junior and senior high school social studies. At present he is the editor and publisher of the *Ideas in Conflict* series and the *Editorial Forum* series.

CHAPTER 1

NO ROOM IN THE MARKETPLACE

NO ROOM IN THE MARKETPLACE

THE PROBLEM IS GETTING WORSE

Catholic Health Association

The following comments are excerpted from a book titled No Room in the Marketplace: The Health Care of the Poor, *published by the Catholic Health Association. This book was the result of a Catholic Health Association special task force study on American health care for the poor.*

Points to Consider

1. Who are the medically indigent?
2. What are some of the holes in the U.S. health care safety net?
3. How do people become medically underinsured?
4. What are the policies of some hospitals toward the underinsured needing care?
5. How have hospitals traditionally tried to cover uncompensated care?
6. What are some of the middle and lower income elderly forced to do to qualify for long-term nursing home care?

No Room in the Marketplace: The Health Care of the Poor, final report of the Catholic Health Association's Task Force on Health Care of the Poor. Reprinted with permission of The Catholic Health Association of the United States, 4455 Woodson Road, St. Louis, Missouri 63104.

Unnecessary human suffering that results from
deficiencies in the U.S. health care safety net makes
equal access to health care an urgent societal goal.

The poor who need health care have had many faces through the centuries: lepers and "possessed" persons in Christ's day; the sojourners of the Middle Ages and then the victims of plagues and epidemics; and more recently, homeless, elderly, unemployed, and uninsured poor persons.

For purposes of this report, however, the poor are "those persons who are unable through private resources, employer support, or public aid to provide payment for health care services, or those unable to gain access to health care because of limited resources, inadequate education or discrimination."

Holes in U.S. Health Care Safety Net

In the United States, large public programs support health insurance: Medicare and Medicaid. Medicare, the federal program for the aged (most of whom are not poor), the disabled, and those who suffer from end-stage renal (i.e., kidney) disease, is projected to cost the federal government about $68 billion in 1986. Medicaid, the federal/state program for welfare recipients, is estimated to cost the federal treasury about $25 billion in 1986. State contributions will increase Medicaid's cost to about $45 billion.

One must remember that *Medicaid does not cover all the poor.* It covers only poor people in the welfare categories: aged, blind, disabled, and Aid to Families with Dependent Children (AFDC); this group represents *only* 31 percent of the poor population. Even in this group, financial and medical vulnerability remains high, since one-third are covered by Medicaid only part of the year and are otherwise uninsured. . . .

In addition, the federal government spent about $20 billion in 1986 on health care for Defense Department employees, their dependents, and veterans.

It is also important to note that public hospitals operated by state and local governments play a major role in the provision of health care. Most often such hospitals are the principal source of care for people who cannot obtain it elsewhere because of an

10

inability to pay, a particular medical condition, or social characteristics that make them undesirable patients. Many are poor, without private insurance, or inadequately covered by it, and ineligible for Medicare or Medicaid.

The Lack of Universal Health Insurance

This patchwork quilt health care system has large gaps in coverage and is far from universal health insurance. One study found that in 1977 (the most recent data available) about 9 percent of the population under age 64 had no public or private health insurance coverage all year. Thus, two groups of uninsured persons exist: the never insured and the part-time insured. Translated into numbers, these percentages indicate that in 1977, 18 million people under age 65 lacked insurance coverage and another 16 million had no coverage for part of that year; the total number without insurance for part or all of the year was 34 million, or 16.5 percent of the U.S. population.

Problem Has Become Worse

To compound these disturbing figures, growing evidence shows that the gap in the U.S. health care safety net has become larger. Since 1979, the number of persons potentially unable to pay for health care has been rising steadily. Between 1980 and 1982, those with family incomes below 150 percent of the poverty income increased by 13.5 percent; the number of inadequately insured, having either no insurance or private nongroup insurance only, grew by 7 percent. Medicaid coverage stayed essentially constant but fell as a proportion of all low income people, from almost 36 to 31 percent. Even more dramatic, persons both poor and inadequately insured increased nearly 21 percent; this population presumably depends more on free care to meet their needs for hospital services . . .

Since our system of health insurance is job-linked, when people lose their jobs, even temporarily, they lose their coverage. Some unemployed or newly reemployed persons without health insurance who are seriously ill or have family members with chronic medical conditions are able to buy only poor coverage at a high price. Many others are unable to buy health insurance at all. They must spend all their savings on medical care, become impoverished, and then rely on the government for publicly

11

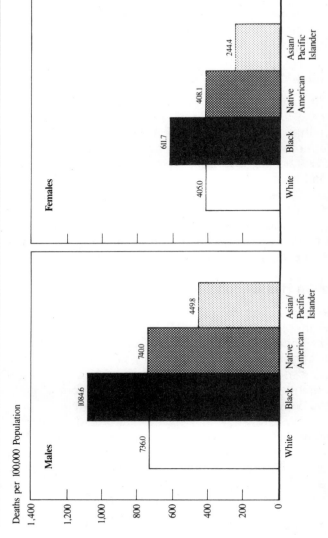

Average Annual Age-Adjusted Death Rates for All Causes, 1979–1981

Deaths per 100,000 Population

Males

White	736.0
Black	1084.6
Native American	740.0
Asian/Pacific Islander	449.8

Females

White	405.0
Black	611.7
Native American	408.1
Asian/Pacific Islander	244.4

NOTE: Death rates for Hispanics are not available. Death rates for Native Americans and Asian/Pacific Islanders are probably underestimated due to less frequent reporting of these races on death certificates as compared with the Census.

SOURCE: National Center for Health Statistics, Bureau of the Census, and Task Force on Black and Minority Health.

provided care. One author aptly noted that this system forces middle class individuals and families into poverty . . .

In stark contrast to the frustration, pain, and even death endured by many sick and uninsured poor persons, a recent news article reveals how some U.S. hospitals have begun to compete for affluent patients by offering luxury suites and hot tubs. The article cites a wealthy patient's experience in a large Midwestern hospital. The patient invited a friend to dinner in his hospital room. "They began with appetizers of herring and pickled vegetables and then moved on to chateaubriand. After dinner they watched 'Amadeus' on (the patient's) large screen television set . . . 'The hospital's room service was just as nice as a fancy hotel,' (the patient said) . . . 'and the room looked like a high-rise luxury apartment.' "

Hospitals that provide luxury suites for wealthy patients often defend the practice by noting that the extra revenues they receive from such patients are partly used to offset the hospital's losses from uncompensated care. "It's a Robin Hood approach," suggests one hospital official. The provision of "designer health care" for the wealthy may enable some hospitals to serve more poor persons and may even be a means of survival for others. Nevertheless, the practice vividly highlights the enormous inequities that characterize the U.S. health care system. Many poor people find it difficult or even impossible to enter some hospitals, but wealthy patients can purchase hospital luxuries that have little or no relationship to their health care needs.

Current Conditions Affecting the Health Care Poor

Several factors explain why health care for the poor is becoming an increasingly urgent concern. For many years privately insured patients indirectly subsidized the cost of caring for the uninsured poor. Hospitals would simply shift costs to their private pay patients to compensate for patients unable to pay for their care, imposing what some have called a "hidden tax."

Recently, however, American business has been aggressively working to restrain the uncontrolled rate of growth in health care benefit premiums. As a result, private insurers are increasingly resisting hospitals' attempts to pass on the "hidden tax" through higher charges. Also, the recent development of a price sensitive market for hospital care demands that hospitals keep their costs under control to remain price competitive relative to other nearby providers and, ultimately, to remain solvent. Under such conditions, few providers are willing to "compete" for the uninsured and therefore costly poor.

At the same time, the federal government and many state governments have aggravated the problem by sharply limiting their commitments to health care programs and by pursuing more stringent payment policies toward providers. Medicaid eligibility standards have been tightened. As a result, between 1981 and 1985 more than one million people were declared ineligible for Medicaid assistance through legislated changes in the rules. Medicaid benefits have also been reduced and payments to hospitals and other providers cut far below actual costs . . .

Medicare also recently adopted stricter hospital payment policies and has increased co-payments, deductibles, and premium costs for elderly beneficiaries. One recent analysis predicts that, partly because of government restrictions on Medicare, 85 percent of all U.S. hospitals will have operating deficits on patient care in 1986. It adds that losses on patient care would be $1.7 billion in 1985, $3.4 billion in 1986, and $2.7 billion in 1987. This situation is likely to worsen as a result of the adopted Gramm-Rudman deficit reduction law, which requires a balanced federal budget by 1991 and would allow the government to hold annual increases in hospital Medicare payments far below the rate of inflation . . .

Not being able to shift costs and facing a price competitive health care market with reduced government support, many hospitals have less means to pay for care of uninsured poor persons just when their numbers have increased. Thus, although poor and uninsured people increased by 21 percent between 1980 and 1982, the volume of compensated care hospitals provided to serve this population increased by less than 4 percent.

This situation has been especially hard on the hospitals that the uninsured poor rely on most heavily: those with disproportionately large numbers of Medicare, Medicaid, and free care patients and small proportions of private pay patients. Recent research has shown that the inability to increase markups from privately insured patients when revenues are squeezed causes hospitals to *limit their charity care.* Even public hospitals have been forced to ration care to the uninsured poor by maintaining "prudent ratios," although at significantly higher levels than private health care facilities. In 1982, public hospitals provided 15 percent of the total volume of care but 47 percent of the total volume of uncompensated care, whereas private hospitals

Dumping Is Documented

Dumping has been documented in New York, Massachusetts, Illinois, Florida and many other states. The issue reached a crisis first in Texas for a variety of reasons. For one thing, the income level at which a patient qualifies for Medicaid is lower here than in any other state except Mississippi. For another, thousands have lost their jobs —and their medical insurance —because of the oil bust and other economic woes. Finally, private for-profit companies own or manage 210, or about a third, of the hospitals in Texas, more than in any other state.

Robert Reinhold, *New York Times*, May 25, 1986

provided 85 percent of all care and 53 percent of the uncompensated care.

It is a simple economic fact in today's price competitive environment that any hospital providing significant uncompensated care must increase prices to recover costs or become financially distressed. When price alone is the key factor for determining which hospitals survive and when government commitments to the uninsured poor are simultaneously inadequate, hospitals providing a higher proportion of indigent care will be seriously harmed.

The preceding discussion should not obscure the fact that *people*, not institutions, ultimately bear the consequences of poverty and lack of insurance . . .

Special Needs of Poor Children and Their Mothers

The inadequate provision of preventive care, especially for children, and prenatal care for women is also a long-standing problem that is worsening. The Children's Defense Fund recently reported that between 1981 and 1982, 700,000 children were taken off AFDC and Medicaid. The percentage of poor children receiving AFDC and Medicaid is lower today than at any time in the past eight years. Only 52 of every 100 poor children receive

15

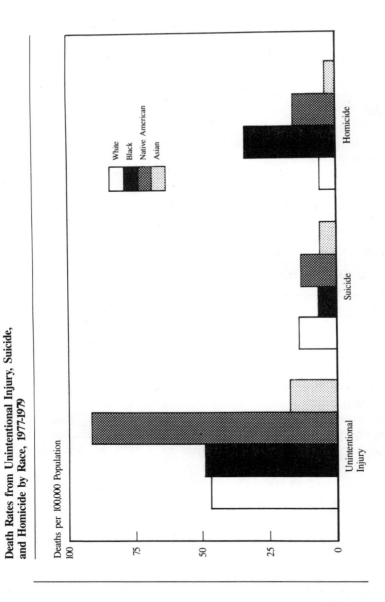

Death Rates from Unintentional Injury, Suicide, and Homicide by Race, 1977-1979

Deaths per 100,000 Population

White
Black
Native American
Asian

Unintentional Injury

Suicide

Homicide

AFDC; only 73 receive Medicaid. Recent data suggest that in 1982 infant mortality worsened in at least nine states, which partly reflects a decline in poor, high risk women receiving adequate prenatal care.

Robbing the Weakest

The Old Testament prophets spoke against all forms of social injustice, with particular attention to the poverty which injustice encourages.
"Shame on you, you who make unjust laws
and publish burdensome decrees,
depriving the poor of justice,
robbing the weakest of my people of their rights"

Isaiah 10:1-2

Plight of the Elderly Poor

Older persons present a special challenge to the U.S. health care system. The incidence and prevalance of both acute and chronic illness increase as one grows older, as does the rate of disability. Some poor persons become old; some older persons become poor, often because of an illness.

Although Medicare has been very important to all older persons, recent increases in Medicare coinsurance, deductibles, and premium costs may be introducing increased financial barriers to hospital care for the poor and near poor elderly. Since 1983, the federal government has been shifting a larger portion of health care costs to Medicare beneficiaries and their families through larger deductibles, greater use of services with coinsurance, and use of services not covered by Medicare. For instance, the deductible which Medicare patients must pay for each hospital stay, except when they are readmitted within 60 days of being discharged, jumped from $400 in 1985 to $492 in 1986—the largest dollar increase in the program's history.

Further, Medicare does not presently pay full costs after a patient's sixtieth day in a hospital; few elderly people stay that long, but those who do often face bankruptcy. About 80 percent of the elderly purchase private "catastrophic" or 'Medi-gap" supplemental insurance or are covered by Medicaid to cover treatment beyond the Medicare limits, as well as most of Medicare's deductible and coinsurance fees. Nevertheless, the premiums paid for the private supplemental policies are increasing. And the remaining beneficiaries not covered by Medicaid face increased out-of-pocket payments for their hospital care and possible destitution should they experience a "catastrophic illness."

Medicare also does not pay for long term nursing home costs, although 1.5 million people (1 out of 20 people over age 65) are in homes and the number is expected to double over the next generation. Medicare covers only nursing home services in a skilled nursing facility (SNF) for people requiring skilled nursing care or rehabilitation in an inpatient setting, but only for a relatively brief period. The average Medicare coverage for SNF care in 1980 was 30 days. Medicare does not cover the lower level of most nursing home care, for which the average length of stay is 456 days. Although much nursing home care is financed with federal and state funds through the Medicaid program, roughly half of all expenditures for nursing home care are made by patients or their families. The plight of the person, usually the wife, whose resources are used for an institutionalized spouse's care, until they have spent down to the point of becoming eligible for Medicaid, is particularly tragic.

About three million more noninstitutionalized elderly persons have disabilities and are cared for by family, friends, and neighbors and most often by the spouse. Although the psychological, monetary, and other costs associated with such care do not appear in insurance or public program statistics, someone must bear them and that person is often ill-prepared to do so.

The need for public and private programs of long term care insurance and ways of paying for it should be carefully examined . . .

The CHA Task Force believes that the unnecessary human suffering that results from deficiencies in the U.S. health care safety net makes equal access to health care an urgent societal goal.

NO ROOM IN THE MARKETPLACE

HEALTH CARE HAS IMPROVED

Peter J. Ferrara

Peter J. Ferrara is an attorney in private practice in Washington, D.C. and is well known as a conservative spokesman on health care issues.

Points to Consider

1. How has the health care gap between the poor and non-poor narrowed over the last 25 years?
2. What examples does the author cite of this narrowed gap?
3. How do cost considerations enter into the access by the poor to health care?
4. What has been the impact of government programs on the poor?

Excerpted from a 1986 position paper by Peter J. Ferrara that was sent to the editor by request.

The literature we have reviewed shows that the health of the poor has improved markedly over the past 25 years, in both relative and absolute terms.

There is abundant literature discussing the health and medical care of the poor in general . . . The literature indicates that the health of the poor has improved substantially over the past 25 years, not only in absolute terms but relative to the rest of the population. The literature also broadly suggests that the poor have sharply increased their utilization of medical services over this period, again in absolute terms and relative to the rest of the population. Much if not most of the low income population may in fact be close to parity with the nonpoor in use of medical services. The poor, however, are still generally less healthy than the nonpoor . . .

Narrowing the Health Gap

A review of the published data and analysis indicates the sharp improvement in the health of the U.S. population over the past 25 years, including the poor. Davis reports that from 1960 to 1983, life expectancy at birth in the U.S. increased 5 years, from 69.7 to 74.7.[1] Blacks experienced more rapid gains in life expectancy over this period than whites. The greatest improvement was for black women, gaining an increase of 7.9 years in life expectancy at birth over this period. Whereas in 1960 a black new born girl had a lower life expectancy than a white new born boy, by 1983 a black new born girl could expect to live over two years longer than a white new born boy. Life expectancy for new born black males increased by 4.5 years over this period, compared to 4.2 years for new born white males.

Age-adjusted death rates for the entire population declined 28% from 1960 to 1983. But Davis reports that the improvement was sharpest for those causes of death which have been most

---

[1] Karen Davis, "Health and the Great Society: Revisited after Twenty Years", Lyndon B. Johnson Library Symposium, The Great Society: A 20 Year Critique, April 18–19, 1985, p. 4; Karen Davis, "Access to Health Care in a Cost-Conscious Society" in Helen Rehr, Ed., *Access to Social-Health Care: Who Shall Decide What?* (Lex, Mass.: Ginn Press, 1986), p. 31.

prevalent among the poor. Death from pneumonia and influenza dropped by 60% over this period, death from strokes fell by over 50%, and heart disease death rates fell by 34%. Deaths from tuberculosis, child birth, diabetes and gastrointestinal diseases declined markedly as well.

Infant mortality was reduced by more than 50% from 1960 to 1983, dropping from 26 deaths per 1000 to 11.2, with equivalent reductions for both blacks and whites. The proportion of low birth weight infants has also declined. Infants weighing less than 2,500 grams dropped from 7.9% of all births in 1970 to 6.8% in 1981.

Butler, et al. note that the improved mortality trends hold for older children as well.[2] For children between ages 1 to 4, mortality rates have fallen from 5.6 per 1,000 in 1930 to 0.8 per 1,000 in 1969 and 0.7 per 1,000 in 1978. For children aged 5 to 14, mortality rates fell by two-thirds from 1940 to 1978, dropping from 0.3 per 1,000 to 0.1 per 1,000. The authors indicate that improvement among poor children has been somewhat more rapid than for the general population, resulting in a narrowing of the gap in mortality rates between poor and nonpoor children . . .

Use of Medical Services

Several writers suggest that the proper standard for equity in use of medical services is that such services should be distributed primarily according to illness or need. This means that individuals would receive more medical services the sicker they are, without regard to income, race, geographical differences in medical resources or other factors.[3] While these writers

---

[2] John A. Butler, Barbara Starfield and Suzanne Stenmark, "Child Health Policy" in Harold W. Stevenson and Alberta E. Siegel, eds. *Child Development Research and Social Policy* (Chicago: University of Chicago Press).

[3] Davis, "Access to Health Care for the Poor," pp. 160, 166; L. A. Aday, R. Anderson and G. V. Fleming, *Health Care in the U.S.: Equitable for Whom?* (Beverly Hills, CA: Sage Publishing Co., 1980), p. 185; Ronald Anderson, "Health Service Distribution and Equity" in Ronald Anderson, Joanna Kravits and Odin Anderson, eds. *Equity in Health Services: Empirical Analyses in Social Policy* (Cambridge, Mass.: Ballinger Publishing Co., 1975), pp. 10–11.

seem to accept such a standard as obvious, it is in fact quite curious. We do not generally distribute goods and services in our market economy according to need, but instead allow goods and services to be bought and sold in the private marketplace, and consequently allocated by their owners in accordance with expressed demand. It is not clear why medical care should be different. It has not been shown that through the usual market mechanisms most people would not be able to obtain the basic, essential medical services, and that government subsidies could not provide for such access for the rest. Once this goal is satisfied, through the market or otherwise, there is no reason why expressed market demand should not be allowed to govern the supply and allocation of all other medical services. This should be especially true of nonessential medical services, which the above standard fails to distinguish. Why shouldn't one consumer who desires more optional care or nonessential care than others be allowed to purchase it, even if he is no more sick than the others? Why shouldn't a person who is more anxious about his medical condition than others be allowed to purchase more care, even if he is no sicker? . .

Is it fair to have medical services distributed according to illness or need if that means that medical practitioners are often required to provide such services without compensation, especially when such services may not be strictly essential? Is it fair to require taxpayers to bear the burden of paying for care that is not essential in order to achieve the standard of equal service distribution? And as suggested above, would it be fair to require some consumers to forego medical services they value most highly if that was necessary to enforce the equity standard of equal distribution?

Nevertheless, the data shows that there have been sharp increases in medical services for the poor over the past two decades and that the pattern of consumption of medical care in the U.S. may now be close to the usually cited abstract standard of equitable distribution. In 1964, the poor saw physicians an average of 3.9 times a year, while the non-poor visited physicians 4.8 times per year and those with incomes over $25,000 visited physicians 5.2 times per year.[4] By 1978, the poor were actually

---

[4] Davis,"Access to Health Care in a Cost-Conscious Society," p. 30; Davis, "Health and the Great Society," pp. 8–9; Davis, "Medicaid and Health Care of the Poor," pp. 6–7.

Government Failure

Many of the nation's religious leaders, including the Conference of Catholic Bishops, are urging expansion of government programs to alleviate poverty.

It's ironic that they are doing so at a time when the failure of government to reduce poverty is increasingly obvious.

Jane S. Shaw, *USA Today*, November 26, 1986

visiting physicians more than the non-poor. The poor saw physicians 5.6 times a year, compared with 4.7 visits for the nonpoor. In 1981, the poor averaged 5.6 visits annually, compared to 4.4 for those with incomes over $25,000. Bane reports that in 1980, low income individuals made 25% more physician visits per capita than the overall population.

Davis reports that in 1964, low income persons were almost twice as likely not to have seen a physician in the previous two years as high income persons. By 1981, the percentage of the population which had not seen a physician in the last two years did not vary with income. Similarly, while in 1964 whites saw physicians at a much greater rate than blacks and other minorities, by 1981 there was no difference by race. The rate of hospitalization exhibited a similar pattern. In the early 1960s, the poor visited the hospital at about the same rate as the non-poor. By 1970, the poor were already visiting the hospital at significantly higher rates than the non-poor . . .

Government Programs

Study may show that counterproductive attitudes and choices result from certain government policies and programs which foster such attributes through unintended perverse incentives and other effects, and therefore that changes in these policies and programs are needed. Failure to uncover the true reality because of a fear of political implications that are speculative and indeed irrational means that the poor could be doomed to

23

continue without the most effective assistance while vast resources may be wasted on poorly designed programs . . .

The enormous amount of resources offered to the poor today through various government programs in fact suggests that lack of resources is likely to play a substantially lesser role in producing the health problems of the poor today than in the past. The data discussed above indicates that most of the poor now are able to obtain access to at least technically proficient medical care to roughly the same degree as the nonpoor, probably due in large measure to government assistance programs such as Medicaid and Medicare. A study by Diana Dutton further suggested that lack of resources per se was no longer the main problem in obtaining necessary medical care. Similarly, it is doubtful that inadequate nutrition of the poor due to lack of resources plays a major role in causing widespread differences in health of the poor as compared to the nonpoor, especially given the enormous resources devoted to government programs aimed at providing food and related assistance to the poor . . .

The Literature

The literature we have reviewed shows that the health of the poor has improved markedly over the past 25 years, in both relative and absolute terms. The poor, however, are still in substantially worse health than the nonpoor, suffering from higher mortality and morbidity.

The literature also shows that medical care use by the poor has increased even more sharply over the past 25 years. Most of the poor, who are covered by Medicaid or some other form of insurance, are probably at rough parity with the nonpoor in use of medical care, even after adjusting for the worse health status of the poor. It is among the uninsured poor where relatively lower use of health care in general continues, after adjusting for health status. However, overutilization of medical care due to extensive insurance coverage has more recently become a focus of concern as a cause of rapidly rising health costs. Consequently, the difference in utilization between the insured and uninsured, including the uninsured poor, may be partly due to overutilization by the insured.

The poor still lag behind the nonpoor in use of preventive care and dental care. Poor children probably also still lag behind their

In a class by themselves

Copyright *USA Today*. Reprinted with permission.

nonpoor counterparts in medical care use, though the gap has narrowed substantially over the last 25 years. Also, young, nonpoor children are the most heavily overserved group in the population, so much of the gap may be due again to overutilization by the nonpoor rather than underutilization by the poor. Some gap may also remain between the poor and nonpoor elderly, though much of this gap may again still be due to overutilization by the nonpoor. It should be remembered that many policy changes are being advocated and adopted today to reduce or eliminate overutilization where it occurs . . .

Issues and Causes

Issues regarding the causes of health problems among the poor and long term effects and consequences of such problems still remain largely unresolved. The worse health of the poor and lower medical care use to the extent it still exists may be due to the lack of resources which plague the poor, and all the problems and factors which result from that. The health problems may also be due to the attitudes, behavior and choices of the poor. The worse health of the poor may alternatively be caused by a tendency for those who are more sick to be driven into poverty by their ill-health, consequently concentrating those in bad health among the poor. The literature does not enable a determination of the degree to which each of these possible causes can explain the health problems of the poor. Each probably still plays an important role.

The sharp improvement in health care and health status of the poor over the last 25 years coincides with the introduction of Medicaid and Medicare, strongly suggesting that these programs were the causes. Yet, only about 40% of the poor are covered by Medicaid, with Medicare not adding many more among the poor, so there must be other causes as well. Health status of the poor had also been improving for years anyway, and many social, cultural, economic, environmental, regulatory and policy factors also appear to have played some role in recent decades. There also has been controversy over the degree to which medical care actually improves health. The available literature does not clearly establish the complete cause of the health improvements for the poor we have discussed . . .

Conclusion

Overall, the literature on health and the poor almost uniformly lacks the recognition that poverty is not permanent for most of the poor. The literature speaks as if those who may be lacking complete health care or insurance or other items today will suffer from these conditions forever. Policy recommendations, explicit or implicit, always seem to be based on the idea that the poor with health problems remain the same year after year. There is no appreciation of the fact that most dependent families graduate from the welfare rolls in two years or less. There is no recognition that many of the uninsured poor are young single males who may have little concern for health care at this point in their lives in any event, especially preventive care, but who 10 years from now will be working husbands and fathers . . .

The literature generally fails to consider that continuing health and nutrition problems of the poor in the face of the massive increase in government assistance to the poor in the past 25 years may indicate the failure of such assistance. It may simply provide further support for Charles Murray's thesis that our social policy overall has worsened, not helped, the condition of the poor.

NO ROOM IN THE MARKETPLACE

PRIVATE MEDICINE IS ABANDONING THE POOR

David Hilfiker

Dr. David Hilfiker is the author of Healing the Wounds: A Physician Looks at His Work, *published in 1985 by Pantheon, and is a physician at two inner-city clinics in Washington, D.C.*

Points to Consider

1. Why has private medicine abandoned the poor?
2. How have the conditions of medical practice fostered materialism?
3. What are "cognitive services" and how are they frustrated in current medical practice?
4. What role has corporate medicine in health care for the poor?
5. Why is the business model for medicine inappropriate for the poor?

David Hilfiker, "A Doctor's View of Modern Medicine," *New York Times,* February 23, 1986. Copyright © 1986 by The New York Times Company. Reprinted by permission.

Medicine is less and less rooted in service and more and more based in money.

Private medicine is abandoning the poor. As a family doctor practicing in the inner city of Washington, I am embarrassed by my profession's increasing refusal to care for the indigent; I am angry that the poor are shuttled to inferior public clinics and hospitals for their medical care . . .

Millions in poverty do not receive Medicaid. More than 30 million Americans lack any kind of medical insurance. Millions of those living in indisputable poverty do not receive Medicaid either because they do not meet the restrictive requirements (it is not enough just to be poor) or because the bureaucratic process is simply too daunting. These poor are sicker and die earlier than the affluent. And the health problems among the poorest of the poor—the homeless—remind one of the third world: active tuberculosis, hernias as big as footballs, untreated fractures and all manner of eminently treatable skin diseases. The statistics on the health of the poor are an embarrassing contradiction to the affluence of our nation.

At private hospital emergency rooms all over this city, it is now standard practice to ship indigent patients who need hospitalization to the District of Columbia General Hospital, the city's only public general hospital. Although the guidelines specify that the patients must be medically stable and able to withstand the transfer, the inevitable delay in securing appropriate treatment has occasionally caused serious harm. These transfers of poor patients from private hospitals to public ones continue to occur despite the fact that the national commission which accredits all hospitals mandates that no patient should be transferred arbitrarily if the hospital he initially visited has the same means for adequate care of his problem . . .

As a private physician, I cannot even admit patients to the private hospital with which I am affiliated unless they have medical coverage or can pay the bulk of the expected fee in advance. What is available for the poor are long waits in the emergency rooms and outpatient clinics of public hospitals, inconsistent care by a succession of doctors-in-training and impersonal service that eventually discourages many from even seeking medical help . . .

Complex Factors

There are, of course, many complex factors that have precipitated private medicine's abandonment of the poor. The urbanization and anonymity of the poor, the increasingly technological nature of medicine and the bureaucratic capriciousness of public medical assistance—all these serve to make private physicians feel less responsible for the medical needs of those who cannot afford the going rate.

But the cause that is probably most obvious to the lay public is singularly invisible to the medical community: Medicine is less and less rooted in service and more and more based in money. With many wonderful exceptions all over the country, American physicians as a whole have been turned away from the ideals of service by an idolatry of money. Physicians are too seldom servants and too often entrepreneurs. A profitable practice has become primary. The change has been so dramatic and so far-reaching that most of us do not even recognize that a transformation has taken place, that there might be an alternative. We simply take it for granted that economic factors will be primary even for the physician.

I do not mean merely to accuse my profession of greediness, though greed exists among doctors as among any other group. Rather, I would suggest that we physicians have been seduced by money; we have been bound by it. Money has become the measure of what we do, the yardstick of our work. Just as if we were in any other business, we physicians have capitulated to the use of economic worth as the determinant of value. In a consumer society such as ours, we doctors are not alone in our idolatry, but our seduction is such a major change from the roots of our profession that it should not go unnoticed.

According to the American Medical Association, the average net income for American physicians is approximately $108,400 a year for 47 weeks of work averaging 56.8 hours each. The usual physician's fee for a physical examination in Washington is $75 to $100, excluding laboratory and X-ray work. Depending on specialty, size of office, efficiency and other factors, about half of the fee is returned to the physician directly; the rest is used for overhead expenses such as office space, ancillary help and malpractice insurance. A thousand dollars is not an unusual surgeon's fee for an hour's surgery plus follow-up visits totaling

Street People

They came in, as many of the men especially do, with feet ulcerations from being on their feet for a number of years. They came in with ulcerations and while we were trying to treat that, they were walking around on their feet getting wet and sometimes frostbitten. We were seeing these ulcers enlarge and enlarge and enlarge until the patients finally ended up with an amputation. So we felt like we could no longer continue to send people who were sick back out on the streets.

The Editors, *Sojourners,* January 18, 1985

---

less than an hour's time. Physicians have become very well-paid servants, indeed . . .

We physicians have not, I think, deliberately chosen to abandon the poor; rather, we have been blinded to our calling by the materialism of our culture and by the way medicine is structured. Many of us entered medicine out of deep altruism, wanting to be of service, only to discover that the daily crush of dozens of sick and needy souls left us exhausted. Under such circumstances, we found ways to detach ourselves from the emotional turmoil of the sick. We may have become physicians desiring to enter deeply into our patients' lives, but we soon discovered that the long lines of patients waiting to be seen encouraged us to be more "efficient" and "cost effective." We discovered that the economic pressure to see 30 or more patients a day did not allow for the kinds of relationships we had envisioned. We learned, too, that our positions of expertise, power and prestige thrust us into positions of authority from which it was difficult to escape . . .

The entrance of corporate medicine into health care has exacerbated all these tendencies. Physicians are now frequently employees of a corporation which is explicitly profit-oriented. Efficiency is now not only important but mandated from above. If the physicians, as healers, do not want to measure their work by its economic production, their employers certainly do, and the attitude filters inevitably down. When the corporate body dictates that the medical care needs to become more efficient in order to increase profitability, there may be discussion about how that goal may best be attained, but ultimately there is little argument about the goal itself.

The fee schedule for medical visits encourages an economic model for patient-physician interactions. In most offices, there are set charges for different kinds of visits—brief, intermediate, extended and complete evaluation—but there are no firm guidelines to determine the fees set by an office for a category. The fee for an intermediate visit, the most common routine visit, may vary from $15 to $50, depending on the office. But there are also no clear criteria for what constitutes what kind of visit, and there is plenty of leeway (by changing the category) for adjusting charges, depending on the patient's financial status, the mood of the doctor or the tenor of the consultation.

The realities of medical economics encourage doctors to do less and less listening to, thinking about, sympathizing with and counseling of patients—what doctors call "cognitive services." Instead, the doctor is encouraged to *act,* to employ procedures. A procedure is anything the physician does to a patient—suturing a laceration, withdrawing fluid from a swollen joint, performing a proctoscopy, removing an appendix. Charges for procedures are a labyrinth of arbitrary rates which are almost independent of the time involved, but they are universally higher than fees for talking with the patient . . .

Something Is Wrong

The monetization of medicine is bad enough for the patient who can afford to pay the going rate . . .

But the business model for medicine breaks down completely when applied to the care of the poor. If we physicians have consciously or unconsciously begun to see ourselves as entrepreneurs, how can we reconcile the need to serve the indigent where little or no remuneration is possible? We are too easily led away from the calling of our profession by the structures we have created.

At some deep level, I think, we physicians know something is wrong. We are invested with enormous trust and confidence predicated ultimately upon our role as healers who place the

"...AND YOU'LL BE UNDER THE CONSTANT SUPERVISION OF POTOMAC SLIM, OUR EXPERT TRAINER!"

patient above our own personal needs. The monetization of medicine strikes at the heart of this trust. As patients gradually recognize that their physician is getting rich from the services rendered, the very core of the relationship is shattered. We physicians must recognize that there is a contradiction between a vocation of service and the inordinate earnings we now command. Though we physicians may deny it even to ourselves, we know it is true.

I do not know if it is possible to begin the return to a medicine based in service. Such a return would not have to mean ascetic monks and nuns delivering care without remuneration—my own yearly salary of $22,000 plus housing is hardly sacrificial. But it would mean a personal and professional commitment to medicine as a vocation of healing everyone who is sick, including the poor. It would mean that physicians base their income on their own need rather than on what the market can bear. It would mean that the truly indigent would be cared for free of charge and that Medicaid—even with all its bureaucratic indignities—be accepted gratefully. It would mean that the poor be charged on a sliding scale based on their ability to pay.

This is already happening in many small nonprofit clinics around the country that are serving the poor; physicians in many of these places are paid amounts equivalent to what other "normal" people earn.

The objection from physicians, of course, is that we are a profession which, by virtue of its long training, intense hours, dedication to patients and self-sacrifice should be well compensated. I would agree that we should be compensated well enough to assure our basic comfort and security, but when we believe that our earnings measure our worth and our dedication, we have accepted the wrong measuring stick. We have stepped away from the basis of our profession. And as we continue to follow this course, ultimately we will abandon the poor.

NO ROOM IN THE MARKETPLACE

THE GOVERNMENT IS ABANDONING THE POOR

Children's Defense Fund

The following statement was excerpted from testimony by Luanne Nyberg before the Senate Subcommittee on Intergovernmental Relations of the Committee on Governmental Affairs. She made this statement in her capacity as Director of the Children's Defense Fund's Minnesota Project.

Points to Consider

1. What health services is the government "safety net" failing to provide?
2. Why is poverty the single greatest cause for the nation's poor infant health statistics?
3. How does the U.S. compare with other western industrialized nations in providing poor women and children with health care?
4. What steps should be taken to improve the situation?

Excerpted from congressional testimony by Luanne Nyberg of the Children's Defense Fund on October 31, 1985.

Fifteen percent of hospitals serving large numbers of poor patients adopted specific limits on the amount of charitable care they would provide.

The Children's Defense Fund is a national public charity created to provide long-range, systematic advocacy on behalf of the nation's poorest children. Through research and policy analysis and advocacy at all levels of government, we attempt to place children's needs higher on the public agenda. The issues with which we are chiefly concerned include child health, child development and day care, child welfare, education, and adolescent pregnancy.

Since its inception, the health division's central concern has been ensuring that all children and pregnant women, regardless of family income, have access to comprehensive, high quality health care. We have sought to achieve that goal by advocating for reforms in governmental programs that finance or provide health care to poor and otherwise uninsured families . . .

The Cost to the Nation of Failing to Care for Poor Pregnant Women and Infants is High

Among western industrialized nations, America stands nearly alone in its failure to ensure that comprehensive medical care is available for all pregnant women and babies who need it. Instead we have developed a health care financing system in which: (1) a family's access to health services depends upon having health insurance; and (2) there exists no basic, residual public or private program for financing health care for all families not insured through the workplace. There is simply no program equivalent to Medicare for financing health services for younger, uninsured families. Instead, we maintain a "safety net" consisting of a patchwork of highly inadequate categorical programs through which millions of children and pregnant women slip annually.

This inadequate approach to financing maternal and child health takes a heavy toll. Families dependent on this volatile, piecemeal public health system are bounced among a series of incomplete and fragmented programs. They are unable to get the early and continuous medical care they need to ensure healthier birth and child outcomes. Moreover, because they are not connected to a comprehensive health care system, they do not receive the type of patient education and counselling needed to promote sound personal health practices. Finally, as we noted above, many providers will actually refuse to treat poor families because the financing mechanisms are not as attractive as private payment systems . . .

Poverty

Experts point to numerous factors that influence the health outcomes of infants. We believe however, that poverty is the single greatest factor. Poverty virtually destroys a family's ability to obtain needed health and related services. The social isolation and absence of supports caused by poverty leave in their wake illness, death and a lifetime of handicaps for a disproportionate number of children born to disadvantaged families.

Poverty is strongly associated with poor health among children. Poor children face an increased risk of low birthweight, neonatal and postneonatal mortality, and such disabilities as retardation, cerebral palsy, autism, vision and hearing defects, and developmental delay.

Many of the underlying causes of death may emanate directly or indirectly from poverty. For example, recent evidence suggests that Sudden Infant Death Syndrome (SIDS), now a leading killer of infants aged one month to one year, is associated with elevated levels of lead in a baby's bloodstream. Elevated lead levels pose particular problems among lower income children.

Moreover, poverty is associated not only with a greater propensity toward illness and handicap but also with a greater severity of illness when illness patterns between poor and nonpoor children are compared. Thus, for example, a cold that afflicts a poor infant is more likely to develop into a deadly respiratory infection because of inadequate housing, poor nutrition, and lack of access to medical care . . .

Infant Mortality

Because our rate of progress in reducing infant mortality is so slow, both we and the United States Department of Health and Human Services have projected that the nation will fall far short of the nation's modest 1990 goals for improving infant health. These goals were set by the Surgeon General of the United States in 1979 and reaffirmed by this Administration in 1984. They include the following:

- By 1990, ninety percent of all pregnant women should receive prenatal care in the first three months of pregnancy.
- By 1990, no more than five percent of infants should be born at low birthweight, and no more than nine percent of infants from any racial or ethnic subgroup should be born at low birthweight.
- By 1990, infant mortality rates should not exceed 9 deaths per 1,000 live births, and infant mortality rates for racial or ethnic subgroups should not exceed 12 deaths per 1,000 live births.

Yet by 1985, it has become clear that these goals will elude America:

- The nation's rate of progress in improving pregnant women's access to early prenatal care is so slow that, unless our annual rate of progress improves by 600 percent per year between now and 1990, we will not meet the Surgeon General's goal for prenatal care. For non-white women, the annual rate of progress must improve by 700 percent per year in order to meet the goal.
- The annual rate of progress in reducing the number of infants born each year weighing 5.5 pounds or less is equally disappointing. Unless the rate of progress improves by 300 percent each year, the nation will not meet the Surgeon General's goals.
- Progress in reducing the number of Black infants who die each year is so slow that the nation would have to boost its annual rate of progress by 170 percent each year to meet the Surgeon General's goal.

The nation's rate of progress in meeting these goals is literally a matter of life and death for thousands of babies. Between now and 1990, 22,000 babies will die in America, primarily because they were born too small to survive. Many more will be handicapped for life. We can prevent 2,700 of these deaths—one out of every eight—simply by making sure that expectant mothers receive adequate prenatal care. Another 13,800 deaths in which low birthweight plays a major role may be reduced if mothers receive early prenatal care . . .

Safety Net

Because private insurance coverage of poor children is so inadequate and the public insurance "safety net" for children is so tattered, access by pregnant women and infants to comprehen-

High Infant Death Rate

The United States has one of the highest infant mortality rates in the industrialized world, according to a Children's Defense Fund (CDF) report issued Feb. 3 . . . By the end of this decade, CDF President Marian Wright Edelman said, the United States "will have spent at least $2.1 billion in first-year costs alone to care for the excess numbers of low-birthweight infants who need extensive medical care and whose tragic situations could have been averted had the nation moved to reduce the incidence of low birthweight."

Burke Magnus, *National Catholic Reporter,* February 13, 1987

sive prenatal and pediatric care (including both medical care, nutritional supplements, and health education) is seriously threatened. As cutbacks and cost containment efforts among both public and private insurers have increased in the past several years, access to necessary outpatient and inpatient care has become increasingly threatened.

• The health needs of the uninsured are putting a heavy cost burden on hospitals: according to information collected by the National Center for Health Statistics as part of its annual National Hospital Discharge Survey, about a half million women who delivered babies in hospitals in 1983 were uninsured.

• It has been estimated that 40 percent of all hospital care for uninsured patients involves obstetrical cases, and that this care adds up to over $1.5 billion per year in hospital charges.

• The number of uninsured obstetric and pediatric cases is so high that according to a recent statistical profile of the source and distribution of uncompensated care in American public hospitals, one out of every two white newborn females will be uninsured. In western hospitals, two out of three white newborn female infants will be uninsured.

Even more ominous is the fact that certain uninsured newborn infants are among the most expensive charity care cases that a hospital can treat, thereby increasing the pressure on hospitals to stop providing services to these babies. At one hospital, for example, high risk newborn infants represented only one percent of all uninsured patients but nearly 20 percent of the facility's uncompensated care charges. An average hospital bill for a high-risk newborn in Georgia exceeds $11,000, and yet high-risk babies are more likely to be born to women who, because of poverty, lack health insurance and are the least able to afford the cost of care. It is the very poorest and least insured babies who are in the greatest need of care and who ultimately may be the least able to get it.

Cost Containment

Given the pressures for cost containment and the large costs associated with caring for medically indigent women and children, there exists a real danger that hospitals will begin to reduce the amount of indigent care they furnish. There are already warning signs of this trend. Between 1981 and 1982, 15 percent of hospitals serving large numbers of poor patients adopted specific limits on the amount of charitable care they would provide. Some hospitals, apparently in response to the high costs involved and the large numbers of children who cannot meet them, have cut back on the newborn intensive care services they will provide to *any* children. These trends indicate that the cost of caring for uninsured children can indirectly constrict the availability of services for all children.

Moreover, a study recently conducted by the American Academy of Pediatrics reveals a substantial increase in the number of patient referrals by hospitals to other hospitals for economic reasons. Of one hundred and eleven hospitals responding to the Academy's nationwide survey, twenty-six percent reported an increased number of referrals to other institutions. Of these half gave low or exhausted Medicaid payments as the reason, while two identified a total lack of insurance as the reason for the transfer.

Reductions in specialized hospital care for women and children are dangerous for even deeper reasons. Between 1965 and 1979, infant mortality rates declined by more than 40 percent in the United States. These dramatic declines were not the result of more preventive health care and the birth of healthier babies, but instead resulted from the development of very specialized

intensive infant care hospital services that now permit us to keep babies alive who would certainly have died twenty years ago. While the number of babies in need of such care is not declining, these special services are in danger of shrinking, and the number of babies whose families cannot afford to pay for them is growing . . .

What reforms are needed within both the public and private health financing sectors to ensure that all pregnant women and infants are able to purchase necessary medical care? What should be the minimum content requirements for any publicly or privately financed maternity care program? How can the nation finance and enforce these reforms? How can we deal with problems relating to the supply and distribution of medical and health personnel? In other words, how do we as a nation get to where we know we should be going?

We believe, furthermore, that we *cannot afford* to simply wait for longterm solutions to these ever-present questions. Today as we meet, 15 Black infants will die simply because the Black infant mortality rate is twice that for white infants. Today state and federal Medicaid expenditures for neonatal intensive care services *alone* will total about $1.5 million—enough to provide comprehensive maternity care to 600 uninsured pregnant women. There is much that we know how to do *now*. While we must devise longterm solutions, there exist many shortterm steps that we cannot afford *not* to take. We have identified many of these actions in our Children's Survival Bill. More immediately, we urge your support for a number of key maternal and child health improvements included in the House and Senate Medicare and Medicaid reconciliation legislation. These improvements include amendments to broaden the scope of services which state Medicaid programs can provide to pregnant women; inclusion of pregnant women from two-parent working poor families in the Medicaid plans of the 18 states that do not now cover these families; extension of the AFDC-Unemployed Parent program for qualified families in all states; and the provision of new funds for adolescent pregnancy services.

This year the nation will spend over a half billion dollars through the Medicaid program just to pay for hospital care for high-risk newborns. By providing comprehensive prenatal care to all pregnant women, we could, according to the Institute of Medicine, cut that expenditure by two-thirds. In this period of economic crisis, this is simply too sound an investment to delay any longer.

EDITORIAL CARTOON

Sanders in The Milwaukee Journal

'Say, aren't you the free market zealots who were protesting Medicare a few years ago?'

INTERPRETING EDITORIAL CARTOONS

This activity may be used as an individualized study guide for students in libraries and resource centers or as a discussion catalyst in small group and classroom discussions.

Although cartoons are usually humorous, the main intent of most political cartoonists is not to entertain. Cartoons express serious social comment about important issues. Using graphic and visual arts, the cartoonist expresses opinions and attitudes. By employing an entertaining and often light-hearted visual format, cartoonists may have as much or more impact on national and world issues as editorial and syndicated columnists.

Points to Consider

1. Examine the cartoon in this activity. (see page 42)
2. How would you describe the message of the cartoon? Try to describe the message in one to three sentences.
3. Do you agree with the message expressed in the cartoon? Why or why not?
4. Does the cartoon support the author's point of view in any of the readings in this publication? If the answer is yes, be specific about which reading or readings and why.
5. Are any of the readings in chapter one in basic agreement with the cartoon?

CHAPTER 2

MINORITY HEALTH CARE

MINORITY HEALTH CARE

INDIAN HEALTH CARE: PROGRESS AND HOPE

Robert Graham

Dr. Robert Graham wrote the following statement in his capacity as administrator of the Health Resources and Services Administration (HRSA).

Points to Consider

1. What is mandated by the Indian Health Care Improvement Act (IHCA)?
2. What was the impact of the President's veto of the IHCA for Fiscal Year 1985?
3. What is the purpose of the Indian Self-Determination Act?
4. What is the charter of the Indian Health Service?
5. Why doesn't the Department of Health and Human Services (DHHS) support a Catastrophic Health Emergency Fund for Indians?
6. Why is DHHS opposed to a federal role for urban Indian health care under Title V of the IHCA?

These remarks were excerpted from testimony by Robert Graham before the Subcommittee on Health and the Environment of the House Committee on Energy and Commerce, April 25, 1985.

Increases in financial and human resources are aimed at strengthening an infrastructure capable of meeting the national goal of raising the health status of the Indian people to the highest possible level.

I am very pleased to be here today to discuss with you and your Committee the reauthorization of the Indian Health Care Improvement Act (IHCA), P.L. 94–437. We consider principles embodied by this Act to be the keystone to the continuing goal to raise the health status of the American Indian and Alaska Native people to the highest possible level.

It was the IHCA which, for the first time, established parity as a benchmark to measure our efforts to reach this goal. It requires the Secretary (of DHHS) to assess the programs established or assisted under this Act to determine additional steps necessary to insure that the health status of and the health services available to Indians are "at a parity with the health services available to, and the health status, of the general population." The determination as to what steps are necessary to continue our progress is reflected in the proposed fiscal year 1986 budget.

President's Veto

Mr. Chairman, given the confusion arising from the President's veto of a similar bill last year, I think it might be useful to review briefly the reasons for his veto, to examine the programmatic effects of the veto, and to comment in general terms on the degree to which this bill addresses the concerns raised in the President's Memorandum of Disapproval.

The President withheld his approval last year for the following reasons: first, he objected to the provision making certain Indians ineligible for certain state and locally provided health care benefits; second, he objected to the unconstitutional mechanism by which the Indian Health Service would be removed from the Health Resources and Services Administration; third, most of the bill's provisions duplicated existing authorities; fourth, the bill would have unnecessarily changed the organizational structure of the Indian Health Service (IHS); fifth, the bill would have increased IHS responsibility for services only peripherally related

Improvements

The Indian Health Care Improvement Act, in conjunction with the Indian Self-Determination Act, represents almost a decade of effort to establish a framework within which Indian people can effectively participate in deciding their role in health programs developed to serve the Indian community.

to IHS's primary mission; and sixth, and by no means least, the authorization levels were excessive.

In his Memorandum of Disapproval, the President made it clear that the veto would have no adverse impact on the ability of the IHS to continue to provide quality health care to American Indians and Alaska natives. Today, over five months into fiscal year 1985, I am pleased to report to you that the broad authority of the Snyder Act [1] has permitted the IHS to continue to provide its entire complement of health care and health care-related services . . .

Health Care Goal

The Indian Health Care Improvement Act is a keystone of our overall efforts. The Act is designed to maintain a health care system which provides high quality health services to the Indian people. Increases in financial and human resources are aimed at strengthening an infrastructure capable of meeting the national goal of raising the health status of the Indian people to the highest possible level and of encouraging the maximum participation of the Indian people in the planning and management of these health systems.

The primary method provided by Congress for the Indian people to exercise maximum participation in the management of these health systems was the Indian Self-Determination Act, P.L.

---

[1] The Snyder Act, passed in 1921, authorized Federal Health & Social Service Programs for Indians.

93–638, which provides tribal governments with the right to take over the operation of most Indian Health Service programs serving them. Nevertheless, the Congress saw that the health systems serving Indians should meet the standards available to the general population before it would be feasible for tribes to assume control. The Indian Health Care Improvement Act was the method chosen by the Congress to bring the Indian health system up to a level comparable to the general population and thus position those tribes, which so chose, to utilize P.O. 93–638 . . .

Significant Improvements

The Indian Health Care Improvement Act, in conjunction with the Indian Self-Determination Act, represents almost a decade of effort to establish a framework within which Indian people can effectively participate in deciding their role in health programs developed to serve the Indian community.

To achieve the intent of the Congress, the IHS, within the framework of self-determination and the provisions of this law, established three precepts:

1. Continue improvement of health programs for Indians in ways that expedite health status elevation and result in health delivery systems which lend themselves to successful local management.
2. Maximize the American Indian and Alaska Native awareness of and participation in all health programs for which they are eligible on the same basis as all others who qualify; and maximize those programs' awareness of the need and efficacy of special efforts to make benefits available and accessible to the American Indians and Alaska Natives.
3. Accelerate development of Indian communities' capacities to staff and manage their own health programs to such extent as they may choose.

During the period that these precepts have been in force, significant improvements in the health status of Indians have been achieved. Nevertheless, disparity remains in the health status of Indians when compared to that of the U.S. general population. Mortality is still 7% higher than that of the U.S. white population, based on 1982 age-adjusted rates.

By David Seavey, USA TODAY

Copyright *USA Today*. Reprinted with permission.

With the foregoing concerns in mind, the Department has developed a legislative proposal which we believe clearly focuses on the goals of the Indian Health Care Act.

Catastrophic Fund

I would like to now turn to some of the specifics . . .

The Department does not believe a separate and additional authorization is required to establish a Catastrophic Health Emergency Fund to deal with extraordinarily expensive illnesses or accidents occurring to Indians served by either IHS or IHS funded programs.

The IHS, as a health system, is able to shift available resources to cover these incidents. The Department supports in principle the effort to rationalize and institutionalize the current IHS efforts to deal with this increasingly important problem . . .

The IHS has been very successful, and is expected to continue to be successful, in assisting tribes in developing the competence necessary to operate and maintain sanitation facilities. The percentage of systems in place and operating at an acceptable level of competence compares very favorably with rural systems run by the general population.

The local control and responsibility of tribes and Indian communities to operate and maintain the water and sanitation systems has been one of the major strengths and sources of success of the program. The proposal would act as a disincentive to tribes currently doing a responsible job . . .

The Department supports extension of section 404 which authorizes grants and contracts with tribal organizations to improve Indian access to the Medicare and Medicaid programs. This provision would be supportive of the Department's efforts to increase third party payments for Indian health.

Urban Indian Health Care

The Department strongly opposes the proposed extension of Title V of the Indian Health Care Improvement Act, Health Service for Urban Indians, and no funds are requested for this purpose in the President's budget for fiscal year 1986. Existing State and community based health organizations currently absorb most of the clinical workload of the urban Indian projects. These projects have demonstrated their ability to generate revenue from other sources. Reduction of direct Federal support should not drastically change the ability of the community to provide linkages that have been established by the urban Indian projects and the funds being generated from other sources by these projects . . .

Uranium Mining Threat

The Department opposes section 703 of the bill which would authorize a study of nuclear resources development health hazards on Indians and Indian miners. Such a study was called for by section 707 of the current law, has been completed and was submitted to the Congress on April 27, 1983. The Department does not believe there is a need for further study of the health hazards of nuclear development activities on or near Indian reservations. Numerous studies have been conducted concerning abandoned uranium mill tailings piles located on Indian land and remedial action begun where appropriate. While a concern, the risk of cancer developing from background radiation in uranium mining or milling occupations is extremely small and other health problems exist on Indian land which pose considerably more risk to the Indian population than radiation. In addition, "A Plan for Diagnosis and Prevention of Illness Related to Nuclear Resources Development on Indian Land" was developed in accordance with section 707(b) and was forwarded to Congress on June 18, 1984 . . .

Low Infant Mortality

Reduction of Indian infant mortality has and continues to be of the highest priority for the IHS and the Department as demonstrated by the fact that the Indian infant mortality rate in 1980–82 is 11.9—equal to the U.S. All Races rate for 1981. While we support the intent of the proposed new section 715, to lower Indian infant and maternal mortality to a rate no greater than that of the general population, we do not support the mechanism proposed. Indian infant mortality for the neonatal period (up to 28 days after birth) is actually lower than for the general population. However, after this period, when the child has left the hospital and returns to the home, the Indian infant mortality rate rises above that of the general population. The ability to affect the rate during this latter period requires a much more complex intervention approach involving not only health care but also environmental, economic and cultural influences. The IHS should not be given the sole responsibility for ameliorating a problem which has considerable non-health aspects.

Because of these complexities, the Department does not believe that a specific five year program would be the most effective use of scarce resources. Instead, the Department recommends continued support of ongoing efforts to reduce infant morbidity as well as mortality.

The maternal mortality rate for American Indians and Alaska Natives residing in the Reservation States for 1980–82 was 7.5 per 100,000 live births. This was lower than the U.S. All Races rate for 1981 of 8.5. There have been relatively few reported Indian maternal deaths in the Reservation States over the past decade, i.e., ranging from one to four deaths per year.

6   MINORITY HEALTH CARE

INDIAN HEALTH CARE: PERILS AND DESPAIR

David Phelps

David Phelps is a staff correspondent for the Minneapolis Star and Tribune. *The following statement was excerpted from three articles on Indian health care.*

Points to Consider

1. What are the funding cuts faced by the Indian Health Service (IHS) budget?
2. In what disease categories do Indians fare more poorly than other components of American society?
3. What criticisms of Indian health have been leveled by the U.S. government itself?
4. What obstacles does the reservation lifestyle impose on Indians seeking health care?
5. What changes in their personal lifestyles could Indians adopt which would improve their health status?
6. Why do some government supplied food items aggravate the risk of heart ailments among Indians?

David Phelps, "Cuts Peril to Indian Health Progress," "Minneapolis Indian Health Board Proves to Be a Winner," and "South Dakota Known for Worst Indian Health Conditions in the United States," *Minneapolis Star and Tribune*, June 1, 1986. Reprinted with permission of the *Minneapolis Star and Tribune*.

In no place in the United States is the health of American Indians worse than in South Dakota.

At 65, with his eyesight failing, Alvin Jackson lives alone in a spartan two-room house deep in the Chippewa National Forest. Among his few visitors are wandering bears and Janet Listebarger, a young nurse with the Indian Health Service.

Without Listebarger's biweekly visits, Jackson, who has no telephone or means of transportation, would have only minimal contact with the outside world and most certainly would do little to treat the glaucoma that has robbed most of the sight from his right eye.

Listebarger is one of two traveling nurses placed on the 26,762-acre Leech Lake Reservation by the Indian Health Service (IHS). Like the doctors and staff assigned to the small IHS hospital and clinic on the reservation in Cass Lake, the 27-year-old Cedar Rapids, Iowa, native is on the front lines of an $865-million-a-year federal agency whose task is huge. But in addition to combating death and illness rates of American Indians, which far exceed those of the U.S. population as a whole, the IHS also faces critical budget battles that could slow its progress and reverse some of its successes. In addition to the mandatory cuts of the Gramm-Rudman Hollings deficit-reduction law, the agency faces a 13 percent reduction sought by the Reagan administration—a reduction that Indian leaders say the reservations can't make up.

Health Disparities

- Despite substantial improvements in health care during the 31-year history of the IHS, American Indians are three times more likely to die by age 45 than all other races in the United States. That is nearly twice the rate for black Americans and nearly four times the rate for whites.
- Deaths caused by liver disease occur four times as frequently among Indians, pneumonia and influenza deaths twice as frequently, diabetes nearly three times as frequently, kidney infections nearly three times as frequently, homicides twice as frequently and deaths caused by accidents—many alcohol-related—more than three times as frequently.
- Providing clinical and hospital services is made doubly difficult because of aging facilities on many reservations, high

54

turnover among doctors and shortages of other medical professionals. While the national ratio of doctors to population is one for every 500 to 600 residents, the ratio on Minnesota's Leech Lake and Red Lake reservations, where most of the IHS physicians are located, is one doctor for every 1,300 Indians.

● Health care also is affected by the economic conditions on reservations, where the general poverty and high unemployment create a sense of despair. Nationally, unemployment among Indians is four times that of the general population. Moreover, reservations often are in isolated, rugged areas where travel is difficult and climatic conditions are harsh.

● The IHS, which is virtually the sole provider of health care funds for most of the Indians it serves, spends about $900 per Indian a year in the Bemidji area, while the national average of private health care expenditures is about $1,500 per person a year.

System is Failing

● In addition, the IHS and Congress have had continuing budget battles with the Reagan administration over proposed funding cuts for the agency. So far this year, the IHS has undergone a 1 percent automatic budget reduction mandated by the Gramm-Rudman law. It faces a 2 percent cut in October, and a proposed 13 percent cut, or $722 million, in fiscal 1987 by the Reagan administration.

"Despite general improvement, much of the Indian population . . . is in poor health relative to the rest of the United States," said the Office of Technology Assessment, an arm of Congress which recently completed a study of the health status of American Indians and Alaska natives.

Rep. Henry Waxman, D-Calif., chairman of the Health and Environment subcommittee which requested the study, said the report describes a system that is failing a people to whom the federal government has a moral and legal trust responsibility."

The IHS was created in 1955 to provide care for nearly 1 million Indians and Alaska natives. It is a branch of the federal public health service in the Department of Health and Human Services and consists of 12 regional offices which operate 51 hospitals and 124 outpatient health centers. Between 50,000 and 55,000

Indians in Minnesota, Wisconsin and Michigan are served by the Bemidji regional office . . .

High Disease Rates

Listebarger and other IHS professionals daily face the problems of poor health among Indians caused by alcoholism, bad diet and a high birth rate, notably among teen-age Indians, whose pregnancy rate is nearly three times the national average. The prevalence of alcohol abuse, according to the recent study, can be inferred from the extremely high liver disease and cirrhosis death rates in almost all IHS areas. Those death rates are more than four times the national level.

Their patients also suffer from heart and liver disease, diabetes and cancer—and some shun treatment. An hour-long trip to a clinic is inconvenient and the turnover in staff contributes to a lack of rapport and comfort between patient and doctor.

Dr. Rick Nicoski, who has worked at the Cass Lake hospital for 10 months, said, "There are more diseases per patient than we saw when we did our residencies (in non-Indian hospitals). There are things we've never seen in our medical training," he said, referring to a recent fatal case of chicken pox in a 3-month-old baby.

The IHS has made notable advances with certain problems. Its programs, for instance, have substantially reduced the incidence of infectious diseases such as tuberculosis, pneumonia and influenza.

But IHS officials remain concerned about the high rates at which other illnesses occur in Indians.

In the Bemidji region, deaths caused by heart disease occur twice as often among Indians as in the rest of the U.S. population, according to the congressional report. Diabetes deaths occur nearly three times as often, the study revealed. The age-adjusted death rate for Indians in the Bemidji region is 1.7 times greater than the national average.

Among the proposals to stretch the IHS dollar is one to restrict eligibility for IHS services to persons who are at least one-fourth Indian. But that is controversial among tribal groups, which always have had the authority to certify who is a tribal member. Such a regulation could affect between 5 percent and 10 percent of the Indian population.

In Poor Health

Despite general improvement, much of the Indian population residing in IHS service areas is in poor health relative to the rest of the United States. In the 3-year period centered in 1981 only one IHS service area, Oklahoma City, had an age-adjusted death rate that was below that of the U.S. all races population.

Office of Technology Assessment, 1986

But Indian health is more than a medical problem. It also is a sociological one that is fed by unemployment, school dropouts, chemical abuse, teen mothers and a general hopelessness about the future. IHS officials and tribal leaders say one can't discuss health improvements without addressing the other issues.

"The problems that plague Indians are the result of not having good work experience," said Alan Allery, director of the Bemidji region of the IHS. "We need more money for health care but we also need jobs and industry; money to turn over on the reservation. Until people have jobs and useful things to do with their time" problems will remain . . .

No Solutions

IHS director Dr. Everett Rhoades, a Kiowa from Oklahoma, agrees that Indians can do much to improve their health care and preaches on that note whenever he has an audience.

"With simple physical conditioning we can get patients off of their medication for diabetes. We know that. It does not cost a single cent and it saves lives . . . The single greatest cause of disease is cigarettes. That's totally correctable," Rhoades told a recent meeting of the Greater Sioux Nation in Sioux Falls, S.D. . .

But Rhoades has no solutions for some of the other problems that show up on mortality charts.

"It's the young that are bearing the brunt of death and they die violent deaths," he said. "The Indian male has a 1 in 20 chance of being murdered during his lifetime. It would be a national emergency if anything like that was going on with polio or diphtheria. We don't know what to do."

What troubles Rhoades, health professionals and tribal leaders is the vicious cycle of reservation life.

Indians drink because there is no work; it helps one forget the despair of poverty and pass the time. But drinking causes liver disease and contributes to heart disease and diabetes. It causes automobile accidents and leads to violence in which Indians fight one another.

Many in the Indian community have adopted the "alcohol culture," said Norine Smith, a Red Lake Chippewa who is executive director of the Indian Health Board, a nonprofit private organization that runs a clinic in Minneapolis partially funded by IHS . . .

The IHS this year will provide tribes with $24.6 million for alcoholism programs, or about 4 percent of its direct health care budget. The agency is seeking a 6.6 percent increase in alcoholism funding for 1987. But the congressional study which examined Indian health care suggested that progress in treating alcoholism has not been very significant. "Despite a long-standing recognition that alcohol abuse is the major health problem of American Indians, there is still no agreement on either the causes or treatment for this problem among Indians," the report said.

Because there is poverty, the diet of many Indians is bad. They eat cheap, starchy foods that are high in calories and low in nutrition. Government-supplied commodities, which are provided as a supplement to their diet, are not much better. The commodities include beans, rice, flour and canned red meats that are high in cholesterol and are packed in high-salt preservatives, both of which increase the risk of heart ailments . . .

IHS Hospitals

The IHS hospital in Cass Lake is about 50 years old. It has 23 beds, fewer than half of which are generally in use. It has no surgical capabilities and emergency cases must be sent to non-Indian hospitals as close as Bemidji or as far away as the Twin Cities. The IHS pays for such care.

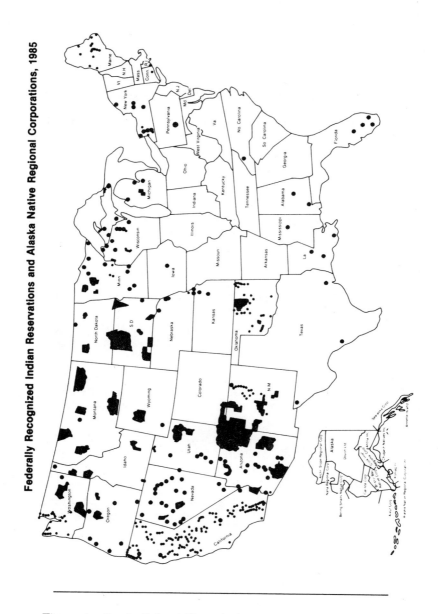

Federally Recognized Indian Reservations and Alaska Native Regional Corporations, 1985

The outpatient clinic at Cass Lakes sees about 100 patients a day. Nicoski, one of four physicians on the staff, said the doctors sometimes handle cases from early in the morning until late in the evening.

Other IHS facilities in the Bemidji region include a 28-bed hospital and clinic in Red Lake and a health center in White Earth. The agency also provides partial funding for tribal-operated clinics at eight locations on Chippewa and Sioux reservations in Minnesota.

One problem which plagues the IHS is staff turnover, especially among physicians. Most of the physicians who work for the IHS do so as part of a program in which their medical-school tuition is paid by the government in exchange for service in disadvantaged areas.

"The doctors we get are good," said reservation chairman Hartley White, the reservation chairman. "But by the time we get them to talk Indian, they're gone."

South Dakota

In no place in the United States is the health of American Indians worse than in South Dakota.

The Sioux tribes of the Great Plains, left to isolated, rugged reservation areas such as Pine Ridge, Rosebud and Cheyenne River, die at a rate twice that of the rest of the U.S. population.

The diabetes death rate is four to five times that of non-Indians, deaths from liver disease and cirrhosis occur nearly nine times as often and sudden infant death syndrome nearly twice as often. The murder rate for Indian males is four times the national rate and for females it is six times the rate elsewhere. Suicides, meanwhile, have increased by 42 percent in the last 10 years.

The facilities in South Dakota are among the oldest and most outdated in Indian country. Patients have to drive hundreds of miles for care; emergency cases sometimes are taken as far away as the Twin Cities. A congressional study indicated that some Indians die because medical help cannot be obtained quickly.

Turnover of professional staff has been very high and until recently doctors would come and leave within weeks . . .

Urban Indians

Even though more than half of the nation's Indians today live in big cities, the Indian Health Service earmarks only a small amount of its budget for their health care. Of the $677 million that the IHS will spend on direct clinical and hospital care this year, $9.6 million will be earmarked for urban programs.

Historically, the government has directed its health efforts at Indians on reservations because of the political and trust relationship between the United States and tribal governments.

More recently, the Reagan administration has attempted to end funding for urban programs on the grounds that those Indians have access to other public health programs that don't exist on the reservations.

But Smith contends that the health needs of Indians are different from the general population and that special programs are necessary to break the grip of "lifestyle-related" problems.

"We have a higher number with diabetes and part of that is related to the use of chemicals. We see obesity, lack of proper diet. It feeds into the poverty thing, the alcohol thing. A weekend drinking binge, for example, elevates the blood pressure." . . .

"If you're going to break those cycles (of drug and alcohol abuse and poverty), you have to start with the youth . . . We give them a support system to keep them in school."

7 MINORITY HEALTH CARE

IMPROVEMENTS IN BLACK AND MINORITY HEALTH CARE

Task Force on Black and Minority Health Care

The following statement was excerpted from the Executive Summary Report of the Task Force on Black and Minority Health Care, *commissioned by Margaret Heckler, Secretary of the Department of Health and Human Services in the Reagan Administration.*

Points to Consider

1. In what ways has the health status of all Americans improved in this century?
2. What is the "biological revolution"?
3. What are the main forms of unawareness by Blacks of their disease risk and how could a reversal of this situation lead to improvements in health?
4. In what settings can patient education take place?
5. How have access to and use of health care services increased for all Americans?
6. What efforts in the non-federal sector can work to improve minority health?
7. How has information on research been disseminated to the Black community?

Summary Report of the Task Force on Black and Minority Health Care, January, 1986.

Programs to increase public awareness about health problems have been well received in several areas. The success of these efforts indicates that carefully planned programs have a beneficial health effect; but the job is not complete and efforts must continue.

Since the turn of the century, the overall health status of all Americans has improved greatly. In 1900, the life expectancy for the United States population at birth was 47.3 years; for Blacks it was much lower—33 years. In little more than three generations, remarkable changes have occurred in health care and biomedical research. As pointed out by the Surgeon General in the 1979 report, *Healthy People,* the leading causes of death in 1900 were influenza, pneumonia, diphtheria, tuberculosis, and gastrointestinal infections. In the first half of the century, improved sanitation, better nutrition, and immunizations brought a drastic decline in infectious diseases. Today, these diseases cause a relatively small percentage of deaths compared to 1900.

Biological Revolution

Knowledge about life processes in health and disease is being acquired at an incredible pace. Because of one spectacular achievement after another, it is predicted that many of the diseases not now curable, will be controlled by the year 2000. This "biological revolution" has placed into the hands of health professionals effective medications, new and complex diagnostic instruments, and treatment modalities not dreamed of in 1900.

Since 1960, the United States population has experienced a steady decline in the overall death rate from all causes. Remarkable progress in understanding the causes and risks for developing diseases such as heart disease and cancer have important implications for the health of all Americans. The decline in cardiovascular disease mortality from 1968 to 1978 alone improved overall life expectancy by 1.6 years. Advances in the long-term management of chronic diseases mean that conditions such as hypertension and diabetes no longer necessarily lead to premature death and disability . . .

In 1983, life expectancy reached a new high of 75.2 years for Whites and 69.6 years for Blacks, a gap of 5.6 years.

63

Nevertheless, Blacks today have a life expectancy already reached by Whites in the early 1950s, or a lag of about 30 years. Infant mortality rates have fallen steadily for several decades for both Blacks and Whites. In 1960, Blacks suffered 44.3 infant deaths for every 1,000 live births, roughly twice the rate for Whites, 22.9. Moreover, in 1981, Blacks suffered 20 infant deaths per 1,000 live births, still twice the White level of 10.5, but similar to the White rate of 1960 . . .

Minorities Are Uninformed

The ability to make informed decisions plays a significant role in influencing the overall health status of Americans. Though not a panacea, health education has been effective in increasing public awareness about actions individuals and communities can take to enhance personal health. The disparity in the death rate between nonminority and minority populations in the United States (Blacks, Hispanics, Asian/Pacific Islanders, and Native Americans) is a compelling reason to investigate how health education can contribute toward reducing this disparity. Because many of the identified behavioral and environmental risk factors associated with the causes of excess deaths among minorities can be controlled, more work is needed to educate minority populations about the risk factors for the six areas identified as having the greatest impact on minority health: cancer; cardiovascular disease; chemical dependency; diabetes; homicide, suicide, and unintentional injuries; and infant mortality . . .

The Task Force has reviewed data suggesting that minority populations may be less knowledgeable or aware about some specific health problem areas than nonminorities. This situation is particularly critical in those areas where minorities suffer a greater burden of illness than nonminorities. For example, Blacks and Hispanics have less information about cancer and heart disease than do nonminority groups:

• Blacks tend to underestimate the prevalence of cancer, give less credence to the warning signs, get fewer screening tests, and are diagnosed at later stages of cancer than nonminorities.

• Hispanic women have less information about breast cancer than do nonminority women. Hispanic women were less aware that family history is a risk factor for breast cancer, and

Prenatal Education

Costs for prenatal education of pregnant women fall far short of the estimated $15,000 required for medical services for each low birth weight infant.

only 25 percent of Hispanic women have heard of breast self-examination.

● Many professionals and lay persons, both minority and nonminority, do not know that heart disease may be as common in Black men as in nonminority men or that Black women die from coronary disease at a higher rate than nonminority women. Hypertensive Japanese women and younger men (18 to 49) are less aware of their hypertension than are the nonminority subgroups, according to a 1979 survey. Among Mexican Americans, cultural attitudes regarding obesity and diet are often barriers to achieving weight control.

Programs to increase public awareness about health problems have been well received in several areas. For example, the Healthy Mothers/Healthy Babies Coalition, which provides an education program in both English and Spanish, has contributed to increased awareness of measures to improve health status of mothers and infants. Also, increased knowledge among Blacks of hypertension as a serious health threat is one of the accomplishments of the National High Blood Pressure Education Program. The success of these efforts indicates that carefully planned programs have a beneficial health effect; but the job is not complete and efforts must continue . . .

Patient Education

The benefits of health education for overall health promotion require a relatively long period of time to be realized. Patient education is a component of health education that requires a much shorter time for its benefits to be observed. Patient education includes increasing a person's knowledge about identified health problems and strengthening the ability to care for that condition . . .

Task Force data suggest that physicians, often seen in clinics or emergency rooms, are the primary source of health information for Black and Mexican American patients. In addition, Mexican Americans regularly seek advice from family members on health matters. American Indians and Alaska Natives living on reservations rely on Public Health Service health practitioners or community health representatives for information. Some Asian/ Pacific Islanders may use traditional healers in combination with physicians. These differences among the minority groups need to be given due recognition in the design and delivery of patient education services.

Patient education programs are particularly critical and needed for several health problems where the impact on minority health is greatest, such as hypertension, obesity, and diabetes.

Patient Education Is Cost Effective

Task Force data suggest that patient education is effective in reducing the cost of health care. For diabetics, it has been estimated that improving self-management skills through education could reduce the complications of diabetes—ketoacidosis, blindness, and amputations—by up to 70 percent, preventing about 50,000 hospitalizations a year. Costs for prenatal education of pregnant women fall far short of the estimated $15,000 required for medical services for each low birth weight infant.

Hospitals in Memphis and Atlanta have had projects lasting more than a decade that offered prevention-oriented education programs geared to early detection, therapy, and continuing follow-up care for diabetics, on the assumption that prevention is effective both in therapeutic effects and in cost. The results have supported this assumption. The Atlanta program has saved an estimated $11 million in costs, and the Memphis program, similarly cost effective, has seen reductions in hospitalizations and diabetic complications. Given the high prevalence of diabetes among Blacks, Hispanics, American Indians, and some Asians, the potential for further savings in dollars and suffering is considerable . . .

Indian Health Service Population by Area Total Service Population, Fiscal Year 1986 Estimate: 987,017

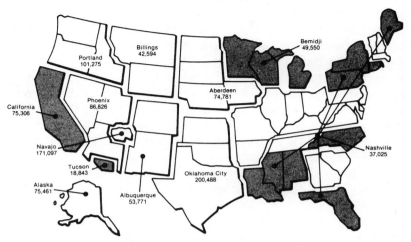

Portland 101,275
Billings 42,594
Bemidji 49,550
Aberdeen 74,781
Phoenix 86,826
California 75,306
Navajo 171,097
Nashville 37,025
Tucson 18,843
Oklahoma City 200,488
Alaska 75,461
Albuquerque 53,771

SOURCE: U.S. Department of Health and Human Services, Public Health Service, Health Resources and Services Administration, Indian Health Service, Population Statistics Staff.

Health Services Used More

The Task Force has reviewed data that indicate low income and lack of health insurance coverage are among the most serious barriers to˙seeking health care. Minorities are disproportionately represented among impoverished Americans. The Department can serve as a catalyst to promote action by private and public entities to address these problem areas more effectively˙. . .

The most commonly used indicators of the adequacy of health services for a population include distribution of physicians, percentage of a specified population who did *not* see a physician during the past year, and average number of visits to a physician. For these gross indicators, data are lacking for some minority groups.

These data do suggest that, in general, availability of health care professionals and utilization of health services for all Americans have increased.

● The rate of increase in the number of physicians in the United States has more than kept pace with the growth of the American population. During the period from 1970 to 1982, the American population grew by 11 percent, while the number of physicians grew by 51 percent. With the exception of Native Americans, most minority populations live in geographic areas where physicians are present. Little is known, however, about the practice patterns of medical specialists and the extent to which they treat minorities.

- In 1970, the percentage of people who had not seen a physician in the past 12 months was 30 percent for Whites and 42 percent for non-Whites*. During the period from 1978 to 1980, these percentages were 23 percent for Whites, 24 percent for Blacks, 33 percent for Mexican Americans, and 20 to 24 percent for other Hispanic groups.
- In 1970, the average annual number of visits to a physician per year was 4.1 for Whites and 3.6 for non-Whites. During the period from 1978 to 1980, the average number of physician visits rose to 4.8 for Whites, 4.8 for Blacks, 4.3 for Mexican Americans, and from 5.1 to 6.1 for other Hispanic groups.

No absolute standards are available for measuring adequacy of health services. Data for nonminorities, however, provide a base against which to compare the use of health services by minorities. In sum, gross indicators of access to and utilization of health services show improvement for the Nation as a whole and for those minorities for whom data are available . . .

Non-Federal Sector

Activities to improve minority health cannot be confined solely to the Federal Government. The participation of organizations at all levels—National, State, municipal, and community—is vital to achieve improved health for minority individuals. State and municipal agencies are increasingly aware of the unique needs of their minority residents. Many localities, in fact, have developed plans to meet the national 1990 objectives for their health care needs.

The private sector can often be a very effective channel for programs targeted to minorities. National organizations con-

---

* The Census definitions of White and non-White were used in 1970. People of Mexican or Spanish descent were coded "White," and Native Americans, Asian/Pacific Islanders, and Blacks were coded "non-White."

cerned with minorities such as the National Urban League and the Coalition of Hispanic Mental Health and Human Services Organizations (COSSMHO) include health-related issues in their national agendas and are actively seeking effective ways to improve the health of minorities. Organizations such as these have a powerful potential for effecting change among their constituencies because they have strong community-level, "grass roots" support.

Changes in health behavior frequently depend on personal initiative and are most likely to be triggered by health promotion efforts originating from locally-based sources. Indeed, community involvement in developing health promotion activities can contribute to their success by giving credibility and visibility to the activities, and by facilitating their acceptance. By addressing health problems that occur within their own communities, minority residents can empower themselves to press more actively for adequate and comprehensive efforts aimed at improving the health of individuals and the community.

Not all minority communities, however, have the ability to identify their own health problems and initiate activities to address them. It is here that the Federal Government's knowledge and expertise in health can join with community and other non-Federal groups to strengthen minority-related health activities . . .

Community Efforts

Results from research sponsored by DHHS are frequently disseminated to the general public or to target populations with the cooperation of national and local media, and community networks.

The National Cancer Institute launched a special cancer prevention awareness program for Black Americans. It began with a mass media effort aimed at increasing awareness among Black citizens that everyone can do something to reduce the personal risk of cancer. The mass media effort will be followed by national and community-based educational activities that rely on strong involvement of traditionally Black organizations.

The National High Blood Pressure Education Program has worked successfully with communities, State and local health departments, industry, and professional and voluntary health organizations to increase health professionals' and the public's awareness about the risks associated with untreated hypertension and the opportunities for effective treatment.

The National Institute on Drug Abuse (NIDA) has encouraged Black organizations to incorporate drug and alcohol abuse prevention activities into their national agendas. NIDA has also provided guidance and support in the development and promotion of national multicultural networks among Black, Hispanic, Asian, and Native American families. One outcome is the development of a network among Black parents and community organizations to stimulate community-based prevention programs in drug and alcohol abuse. This model for a "grass roots" prevention program is being replicated in a select number of cities across the country.

THE BLACK HEALTH CARE DISASTER

Harvey Webb, Jr.

Dr. Harvey Webb, Jr., is the executive director of Constant Care Medical Center in Baltimore, Maryland.

Points to Consider

1. Describe some of the physical conditions of urban poverty.
2. What are the main health status barometers for blacks?
3. Why does the author refer to Secretary Heckler's Task Force as "ominous"?
4. How did the Community Health Center Program originate?
5. What are the special advantages of these centers?

Harvey Webb, Jr., "Community Health Centers: Providing Care for Urban Blacks," *Journal of the National Medical Association,* Vol. 76, No. 11, copyright © 1984, pages 1063–7. Reprinted by permission of the National Medical Association.

It is a national disgrace that the infant mortality rate in some urban, predominantly black areas is higher than the rate in some underdeveloped countries.

Close your eyes for a minute and picture it—a low-income, urban black neighborhood. It is a community of shade trees and aging brick row houses, remnants of a more prosperous time 50 years ago or more. The look is typically Baltimore. With little imagination, however, you can transpose the scene to the baked-out slums of Los Angeles—flat, crumbling, stucco cracker-boxes and, here and there, a forlorn scraggly palm tree. Or you can move to the sidewalks of Harlem or Philadelphia or Washington, DC, where squalor exists in the shadow of the White House. It shouldn't be hard to imagine, because poverty, illness, and disease are found throughout the nation. And blacks are suffering everywhere.

Smell the stench of stale urine in the gutters. Hear the frustrated screams of neglected children, already incapable of healthy anger. Walk gingerly among the piles of broken glass in the streets and vacant lots. Wade through the garbage in the alleys. Watch out for rats!

Peer through the basement window of that boarded-up house over there. You might see a junkie shooting up, trying vainly to escape his life. See the wino sleeping in the doorway. Greet the fat lady sitting on the steps. Take her blood pressure and be shocked. And cry for all those pretty, bright children with the chronic runny noses, nervous stomachs, and lead in their bloodstreams.

To be poor and black in America today is to know personal pain and physical discomfort. It is living uncomfortably close to the untimely death of acquaintances and family members. It is enduring problems like cancer and hypertension. It is, often, struggling along as a single parent against hunger, cold, unsafe neighborhoods, and the lack of adequate health care.

Dead-end jobs, unemployment, teenage parenthood, short life expectancy, bread lines, stress, and insecurity—these are common in the poor urban black community. In 1967, the National Advisory Commission on Civil Disorders reported that "the residents of the racial ghetto are significantly less healthy than most other Americans. They suffer from higher mortality rates, higher incidence of major disease and, in recent years, lower

Cancer Rate

The overall rate of increase in the incidence of cancer among blacks is twice that of whites; the rate is as much as fifteenfold with some of the most fatal cancers, including cancer of the colon and rectum. Hypertension kills blacks 15 times more frequently than whites. In the workplace, blacks have a 37 percent higher risk of occupationally induced disease and a 20 percent higher death rate from occupation-related diseases.

John Conyers, Jr., *Washington Post*, December 30, 1983

availability and utilization of medical services. They also experience higher admission rates to mental hospitals." Early in 1984, the Children's Defense Fund issued a report titled *American Children in Poverty*. This report presents new statistics on an old injustice: blacks are three times more likely to be poor than whites, one in two black children is poor, one in every six black Americans is unemployed, one in two black youths is unemployed, and only 61 percent of all black men are now in the labor force.

Barometers

At Constant Care Medical Center in Baltimore, Maryland, a myriad of serious health problems experienced by blacks are seen. Three of them stand out as most alarming. They are barometers of community health, and they demonstrate conclusively that there is no equal access to health care in this nation today. These health status barometers are cancer, hypertension, and infant mortality.

Cancer

A 1982 report titled *Cancer Facts and Cancer Figures*, published by the American Cancer Society, states that studies conducted over several decades show that the cancer incidence rates for blacks are higher than for whites, and that blacks also have a higher death rate from cancer than whites. "In 1982," states the report, "the overall cancer incidence rate for blacks went up 8 percent, while for whites it dropped 3 percent." Cancer mortality has increased in both races, but the rate for blacks is greater than for whites. In the last 25 years, the cancer death rate for whites has increased 9 percent, whereas the black rate has increased 34 percent. Twenty-five years ago, the rates were the same.

One black in four suffers from some kind of cancer. According to the American Cancer Society, "the cancer sites where blacks have significantly higher increases and incidence in mortality rates include the lung, colon-rectum, prostate, and esophagus." Esophageal cancer, long considered a disease mainly of men, declined in whites but increased dramatically in blacks, both men and women. The report also states that "the incidence of invasive cancer of the uterine cervix dropped in both black and white women, but the incidence in blacks is still more than double that in whites."

Survival rates for cancer patients diagnosed between 1967 and 1973 were compared. More whites than blacks had cancer diagnosed in early, localized stages, when the chances of cure are best. In addition, a recent American Cancer Society survey conducted by a black-owned consulting firm showed that urban black Americans tend to be much less knowledgeable than whites about cancer's warning signals and less apt to see a doctor if they experience any of these symptoms. The blacks interviewed knew little about the three cancers that have seen sharp increase in mortality—colorectal, prostate, and esophageal. The survey also showed that blacks tend to underestimate both the prevalence of cancer and the chances of cure.

In both studies, most of the differences between whites and blacks were attributed to economic, environmental, and social factors, rather than to inherent biological characteristics. A higher percentage of blacks than whites are in low socio-economic groups residing in old industrial neighborhoods; therefore, their risk of exposure to industrial carcinogens is increased. Also, the fact that blacks are frequently deprived of health education works against their being alert to the symptoms of cancer and obtaining early diagnosis and treatment.

74

When a community has a well-run, widely accepted, heavily used community health center in its midst, the residents have a fighting chance against cancer. Periodic checkups, frequent and deliberate health education sessions, and continuous references to the early warning signs of cancer, as well as appropriate, timely treatment make substantial inroads on cancer. The community health center, in fact, could become the nation's most effective offensive weapon in the black community's war on cancer.

Hypertension

Each year high blood pressure causes hundreds of thousands more deaths from heart attacks and strokes for black Americans than for white Americans. Heart attacks and strokes in blacks are estimated to be 66 percent higher than for whites. Blacks have high blood pressure at one and one-half times the rate of whites.

High blood pressure is of special concern for low-income blacks; it is present in 25 percent of the population at age 17 and in 40 percent of the population over age 65. Less than 10 percent of these blacks receive adequate medical care, as a common health care practice in the low-income black communities is to seek only episodic health care in a hospital emergency room. As in the case of cancer, many black hypertensives do not seek medical care until it is too late. To make matters even worse, hypertension is a "silent killer" often with no symptoms to motivate its victims to seek help. The estimated prevalence of undiagnosed elevated blood pressure for blacks over 18 in the State of Maryland is 78,370, or 14 percent of the total nonwhite population.

The U.S. Department of Health and Human Services reports that 50 percent of all men aged between 55 and 64 years suffer from high blood pressure as compared with only 30 percent of all white men. In all other age groups, hypertension is also higher for blacks than for whites. The survey indicated that men under 50 years of age, especially black men, frequently fail to have their blood pressure measured because they have no one constant source of medical care. When they do have their blood pressure measured, they are not given specific information about high blood pressure or its treatment. Further, many blacks have the erroneous belief that high blood pressure is caused by nervous tension, occurring only when they feel tense. Some other reasons why high blood pressure goes untreated are the lack of support from family and friends, the lack of motivation to change unhealthy nutritional habits, and the high cost of medication. As in the case of cancer, the best treatment for hypertension is health education and continuity of care. Community health centers have the potential to greatly reduce the prevalence and severity of hypertension among all black Americans . . .

Infant Mortality

It has been known for the past 20 years that the infant mortality rate is at least 85 percent higher, almost double the rate, for black babies than for white babies. Black babies are more likely to die because black mothers, who are more likely to be poor, simply cannot afford the prenatal care that would save their infants' lives. Babies born to women who receive late or no prenatal care are three times more likely to die in infancy as those babies born to women who receive adequate health care. Black babies in some medically underserved areas are dying at a rate almost four times the white infant mortality rate. Moreover, according to a report titled *The Widening Gap,* issued by the Food Research and Action Center in Washington, DC, the gap between black and white infants is growing.

Another reason for early infant death is malnutrition of the mother while the baby is in utero and of the baby itself after birth. Also, some people are ignorant of life-preserving sanitation and safety practices that others take for granted. This problem is most serious in the case of adolescent mothers, and adolescent pregnancies are epidemic in the black community. Prenatal and postnatal counseling by health providers who understand the problem and *care* greatly increases a baby's chance to live. Family planning is also crucial, yet it is still unavailable to many urban teens.

It is a national disgrace that the infant mortality rate in some urban, predominantly black areas is higher than the rate in some underdeveloped countries and even in a few war-torn nations like El Salvador. Community health centers can help bring about a substantial reduction in infant mortality in their patient populations . . .

We Know the Problem

All over the nation and around the world, when assistance reaches people it makes an impact and health statistics improve. It becomes ominous then that the Reagan-appointed Secretary of Health and Human Services is commissioning still another study to probe the causes of black infant mortality. We already know why the incidence of infant mortality, cancer, and hypertension is so much greater in the black community. The reasons are inadequate health care, poverty, and a lack of health education that the majority population receives as a matter of course.

We know *why* blacks are unhealthier. The question is, when is something going to be done about it?

Community Health Centers

All of these health disparities could be remedied if adequate health care were available. Community health centers have been bright spots on the bleak horizon. Community health centers are a product of the Great Society, which attempted to bring health care to the deprived. The community health center gives area residents accessible, empathic treatment, and offers a wide variety of health care services under one roof. Community health centers are located in low-income, medically underserved areas. However, since the Reagan administration took office, grants to community health centers have been steadily eroding . . .

Now all income groups have another health option—the community health center. Fifteen years ago, as a priority of the War on Poverty, the first community health centers began to operate in row houses, storefronts, and schools. Their mission was to reach the heretofore unreachable—the medically indigent who took their diseases for granted and died young. Since their beginnings, community health centers have come a long way. The quality of their care has always been excellent; now, however, they are combining business with altruism. They are still in a better position than any other health care entity to reach the medically underserved . . .

Unlike many hospitals, emergency rooms, and private practitioners, community health centers give preventive and comprehensive care. Community health centers emphasize wellness, not sickness. It is their aim to keep patients out of the hospital. They discourage unnecessary office visits and unnecessary diagnostic tests. They strive to bring the hospital emergency room back to its ideally intended use of treating bona fide emergencies and not crises brought on by neglect. Their success has been considerable; repeatedly, community health center patients have been shown to average fewer physician visits, fewer trips to the hospital emergency room and shorter hospital stays. The centers' service is also inexpensive. Care delivered at a community health center costs 50 percent less than the same care delivered in a hospital outpatient department . . .

Community health centers provide health care to patients not welcomed by any other provider. Hill-Burton Act * of 1946 and Medicaid notwithstanding, poor black patients do not truly have the freedom to obtain the comprehensive, high-quality, constant care that they need. Community health centers are the answer. Working side-by-side with private practitioners and hospitals as a partner, not a competitor, there is no end to what they could accomplish for the healthier lives of American blacks.

* Note: The Hospital Survey and Construction Act, more popularly known as the Hill-Burton legislation, was passed in 1948 and provides funds for hospital construction in return for guarantees of care for the poor.

EXAMINING COUNTERPOINTS

This activity may be used as an individual study guide for students in libraries and resource centers or as a discussion catalyst in small group and classroom discussions.

The Point

The federal government should not pick up the cost of medical care for illegal aliens to save money for New York and other large cities. Granting illegal aliens access to Medicaid is a dangerous erosion of the federal government's ability to control illegal immigration. To open up the Medicaid program to aliens illegally in the United States opens the door to their participation in other welfare programs and provides further attraction to immigrate or stay here illegally.

The Counterpoint

Reduced Medicaid help for the undocumented means that they defer medical care for as long as possible, then show up for treatment at already overburdened locally run public hospitals and clinics. New York City, for example, now absorbs an estimated $25 million in unreimbursed Medicaid payments for illegal aliens.

All undocumented aliens should be entitled to Medicaid since illegal immigration reflects the Federal Government's failure to control the borders. That may overstate the issue, but the practical case seems irrefutable for helping all who are pregnant, young children, aged, blind or otherwise disabled.

A Federal tax dollar spent to give them rational health care would automatically save many more tax dollars eventually necessary to compensate for their neglect.

Guidelines

Social issues are usually complex, but often problems become oversimplified in political debates and discussion. Usually a polarized version of social conflict does not adequately represent the diversity of views that surround social conflicts.

Examine the counterpoints above. Then write down other possible interpretations of this issue than the two arguments stated in the counterpoints above.

CHAPTER 3

HEALTH CARE ALTERNATIVES
FOR THE POOR

HEALTH CARE ALTERNATIVES FOR THE POOR

A STRONG FEDERAL COMMITMENT IS NECESSARY

James L. Rout

James L. Rout is Chair of the Board of Commissioners of Shelby County, Tennessee.

Points to Consider

1. What level of government has traditionally borne the ultimate responsibility for providing for the medically indigent?
2. What has been the main limitation to funding for local authorities to meet the increasing demand?
3. How does NACo's (National Association of Counties) platform document spell out the funding mechanism they would like?
4. What does NACo believe the shortcomings of risk pooling to be?

Excerpted from hearings before the Intergovernmental Relations Subcommittee, U.S. Senate Committee on Governmental Affairs, June 26, 1986.

As a national problem, the issue of access to care demands a national solution.

Assuring access to needed health care for those who are currently denied it is a pressing national priority.

The National Association of Counties (NACo) has long been interested in the problem of access to health care in the United States. Its interest derives from both a commitment to the health and well-being of the constituents of county governments and from a concern over the escalating costs to counties in providing care to those who have nowhere else to turn for assistance. For the indigent and the poor, access to health care frequently means access primarily through the portals of county programs or financing.

Historically, counties have been the providers of last resort for the health care of the poor and indigent. We operate an extensive network of county hospitals and public health services, clinics and nursing homes which directly deliver treatment to people who are uncovered by insurance and lack the means to finance their own care. In Memphis, Shelby County, Tennessee, we put almost $60 million in our two nursing homes and public hospital to make up the financial shortfall that results annually due to those patients who cannot pay or can pay only a small portion.

We know the problem of access to health care, because it is at the county level that the "rubber hits the road." We see the problem every day—in very human terms. Uncompensated care is a major social dilemma facing our nation. And the problem is not getting better. It is worsening.

According to a report just released by the Catholic Health Association,

"Growing evidence shows that the gap in the U.S. health care net has become larger. Since 1979, the number of persons potentially unable to pay for health care has been rising steadily. Between 1980 and 1982, those with family incomes 150 percent below (sic) the poverty income level increased by 13.5 percent; the number of inadequately insured, having either no insurance or private nongroup insurance only, grew by 7 percent. Medicaid coverage stayed essentially constant but fell as a proportion of all low income people, from almost 36 to 31 percent. Even more dramatic, persons both poor and inadequately insured

83

increased nearly 21 percent; this population presumably depends more on free care to meet their needs for hospital services."

These are people, 37.1 million of them, Mr. Chairman, who end up in hospital emergency rooms seeking non-emergency care. These are the expectant mothers who delay vital prenatal care; the homeless; the unemployed; the mentally ill; the aged too proud to seek help until desperation drives them to it. Every day in every county in America the problem of lack of access to adequate health care reveals itself in stark human terms.

Counties Cannot Cope

But, what are counties to do? Despite the legal theory of government having "deep pockets" and an unlimited ability to pay, the fact is that county treasuries are hard pressed to pay the bills of indigent and poor patients. County hospitals tend to be old facilities needing major repair. But we are constrained in our ability to pay or to capitalize renovations and expansion of facilities by factors beyond our control. We cannot continually replenish our resources because our taxing power is too often constitutionally limited or stretched to the breaking point. Our taxpayers, through their local ballot, have sent us the clear message that their willingness to pay has practical limits.

NACo believes that the problem is national in scope, despite regional variations in severity. And, as a national problem, the issue of access to care demands a national solution. That is why our Association's fundamental policy document, *The American County Platform,* argues for a Federal system of financing health care. To quote the Platform, we believe,

"The financing mechanism must be a broad-based national tax system. Delivery of care should not be permitted to reflect the widely varying capacities of local economies to finance health care services. Access to basic care should not be a function of the local economy or income. . . . The program must provide a required basic level of coverage to all residents of the United States. . . . The financing method must be at a level of spending responsive to health needs and to the rate of inflation, neither freezing expenditures at current levels nor leading to excessive future investment in health services . . ."

National Right to Health Care

"The bottom line is not urban centers, health centers, and migrant health centers. The bottom line is national health care as a right, as a basic right to every American!"

The Rev. Arturo Fernandez, currently of Fresno, California, and for thirteen years an urban minister in the barrios of Houston, Texas, spoke these words during a presentation at a United Methodist Hispanic Health Care Policy Consulta.

Lee Ranck, *Engage/Social Action*, October 1979

Risk Pooling

We believe this Subcommittee should carefully review the experience with risk pooling in those states which have enacted such legislation. It may be that such pools do not provide the anticipated results because of prohibitive participation costs for intended beneficiaries. There is some data which suggests that underutilization may not make the dance worth the dime.

Florida is a case in point. One of the 9 states currently operating risk pools, Florida enacted its comprehensive health insurance statute in 1982. By the end of 1985, only 257 policies had been sold. Indiana had only 3,069 enrollees in its plan as of April, 1984—four years after enactment. Similar figures in the other states suggest that risk pooling will leave us a long way from providing coverage for the 37.1 million Americans who have fallen through the cracks in our social safety net.

If the pool only attracts those individuals at high risk, the adverse selection factor could defeat the best of cost containment efforts. In general, a community-rated system that spreads risk across a larger population seems more desirable than one which concentrates high risk individuals in a health care ghetto.

We recognize that, in your home state of Minnesota, Mr. Chairman, over 10,000 people have benefitted from the state-run pool. But even with this success story, it must be acknowledged

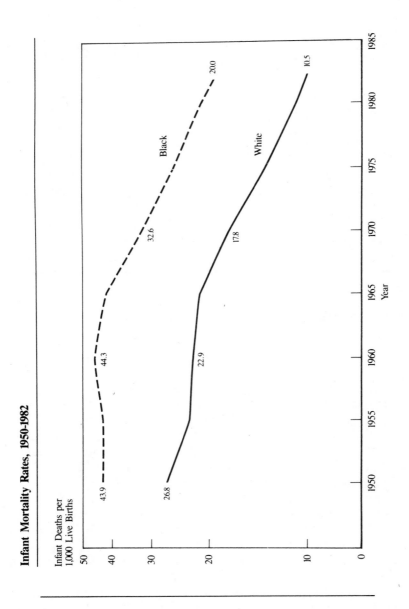

Infant Mortality Rates, 1950-1982

that the pool only reaches a small percentage of those who need coverage. With a $1,000 deductible and premiums running to $1,200 per year, only those with the means to participate can do so and presumably those with the highest health risk will have the greatest incentive to join. Perhaps that is why in Minnesota substantial losses have been incurred by the risk pool in every year since its inception—losses ranging from a ratio of 236% in 1981 to 151% in 1984. (Loss ratio is the percentage of claims incurred to earned premiums.) We agree with your assessment that "Obviously, this alternative is not for everyone, but it surely has made a difference for many Minnesotans." We believe it is important to keep in mind that the risk pool is not a panacea, but is part of a larger whole, each part of which is important to the goal of achieving the stated objective of this legislation.

Dumping

One wonders, as well, at the impact of a risk pool on traditional insurance coverage. Would the existence of such a pool tempt third-party payors to exclude certain coverage or skim low-risk clients, leaving the pool to absorb ever-increasing numbers of high cost beneficiaries? In Wisconsin, which has a risk pool modeled after Minnesota's, a 1984 survey of subscribers indicated that 97% were eligible to participate in the plan because they had been rejected by two or more insurers and 42% rated their health as less than good. Not surprisingly, Wisconsin's pool failed to achieve its objective of becoming self-sufficient after three years and has had to increase its premiums to as much as $1,836 per year. Such experiences prompt us to ask what incentives a risk pool provides for expanding opportunities for the uninsured to become part of the traditional insurance network? What assurances can be made that insurors will not "dump" more high-risk subscribers into the pool? . . .

Financial Problems

Many of our counties are faced with serious financial problems. Where property tax revenues have dropped through devaluation of land, where voters have refused to approve increased levies, or where levies have bumped up against constitutional limitations, counties have been forced to reduce their work forces to meet their fiscal obligations or absorb cutbacks in Federal assistance. We recognize the humanitarian instincts which prompt proposals to continue group coverage of laid-off workers and their families, but there is a price tag to such initiatives. Any mandate of this type, without Federal participation in the costs, may prove truly burdensome for financially-strapped counties. And such counties are the very ones most likely to confront the problem because their revenues cannot support continuation of existing work forces.

In summary, NACo views S. 2403 (the Access to Health Care Act of 1986) as a positive and creative contribution to the dialog over the issue of providing access to health care for the uninsured and underinsured. We will be reviewing your proposal in greater depth at our forthcoming Annual Conference in mid-July. But in the absence of any change in policy by our membership, we must reaffirm our belief that national financing of our health care system is the most direct and preferred approach to assuring access to health care for the people of our nation. That remains NACo's long-term objective, despite the current temperament which weighs against it. In that regard, we endorse your view that "as long as the objective is not forgotten and the process to get there is not forsaken" then stopgap measures remain worthy of our consideration.

HEALTH CARE ALTERNATIVES FOR THE POOR

WE SHOULD MINIMIZE THE FEDERAL ROLE

Self Insurance Institute of America (SIIA)

The following statement is by the Self Insurance Institute of America, Inc. (SIIA), a national association of over 600 members including employers, third-party administrators, reinsurance companies and other interested parties dedicated to the improvement of the self-insurance industry.

Points to Consider

1. What would the bill under consideration (S. 2403) mandate in terms of benefits for laid-off employees?
2. Why does the SIIA believe that additional federal controls would create less rather than greater health care coverage?
3. How does the SIIA perceive the benefits of the Employee Retirement Income Security Act (ERISA)?
4. How would the legislation exacerbate the problem of rising costs?
5. How would the legislation encourage some employers to drop their employer-sponsored benefit plans?

Excerpted from the testimony of the Self Insurance Institute of America in hearings titled *The Access to Health Insurance and Health Care Act of 1986* (S. 2403) before the Senate Subcommittee on Intergovernmental Relations of the Committee on Governmental Affairs, June 26, 1986.

This private system is working well and should not be burdened with costly new requirements which would inhibit its continued growth.

The Self Insurance Institute of America, Inc. (SIIA) appreciates the opportunity to express its views on S. 2403, "The Access to Health Care Act of 1986", which would, among other things, require that employer-sponsored group health plans provide health insurance benefits for four months for employees who are laid off and their dependents.

In brief, SIIA supports the present system of voluntary, employer sponsored health plans which provide benefits to millions of employees. These plans are tailored to meet the varying needs of employers and employees in accordance with the unique requirements of the employer-employee relationship. SIIA opposes federal controls which would mandate special coverages because they would increase already spiralling private sector health costs and limit flexibility in plan design. Such action will impact adversely on the private voluntary system and will create *less* rather than greater coverage. Indeed such legislation would be particularly burdensome for smaller employers who may have to lower wages or eliminate group coverage altogether.

Federal Mandates Will Reduce Coverage

For over 50 years employers have taken the initiative on a voluntary basis to provide employer-sponsored, and in many cases, employer paid health benefits to their employees. Recently, the President signed into law legislation which mandated that employer sponsored group health plans, whether insured or self-insured, must allow previously covered spouses and dependents of former employees to elect to continue health coverage. On the heels of this new law, Congress is now considering yet another Federal law, S. 2403, which would intrude once again into the private health care system by mandating that additional benefits be provided under private plans.

This law requires, among other things, four months of employer paid health benefits for laid off workers. This latest mandate will make it even less attractive for employers, particularly small employers, to continue to provide employer-sponsored health benefit programs. In short, as the Federal

The Real Enemy

I have concluded that government is not the enemy, the enemy is people who depend on it for too many solutions. We ignore alternatives already at our elbows —for instance, pursuing proven privatized service, and I do understand the limitations surrounding contracted and government service. Our appetite addiction and love of government-delivered services can be modified.

I think that while the business world is trying to keep up, even get ahead—the government world, particularly human services, will never catch-up. There have never been enough means even in good economic times to do all the good and fund all the programs that are desired.

D. Michael Stewart, Commissioner, Salt Lake Commission, November 29, 1986

government continues to mandate the inclusion of health care benefits, we are concerned there will be a deterioration of this voluntary system and employers will elect to discontinue providing employer sponsored (paid) health care coverage. Thus, we submit that S. 2403 is not in the best interest of employees, dependents of employees, employers, providers of health care, and the general population.

Private Voluntary Health Care System Works Effectively

The vast majority of our population is in fact covered by some form of health care, whether provided through private group funding arrangements or through the Government. Private sector plans are designed to meet the specific needs and financial resources of employers and employees. Employers now spend an estimated $100 billion each year on health care for their employees. As employer sponsored health care plans have multiplied, basic medical coverages have expanded, and new programs have been added to cover medical expenses beyond the traditional exposures. For example, dental protection as well as other forms of health care protection such as vision care, long term and short term disability are now provided under many employer sponsored health care programs. Moreover, ERISA (Employee Retirement Income Security Act) gave employers an opportunity to provide uniform benefit plans without state government interference when they elect to self fund the benefits rather than use the services of a commercial insurer. ERISA's broad Federal preemption provisions, which preclude state regulation of welfare benefits plans, implicitly reflects Congress' rejection of minimum standards for such plans, including coverage. This private system is working well and should not be burdened with costly new requirements which would inhibit its continued growth.

S. 2403 will erode the concept of voluntary employer sponsored programs. Although the concern of government to expand the availability of health insurance to those who are not presently covered is understandable, we do not believe the answer to this problem lies in mandating the inclusion of such coverage in private plans. In effect, S. 2403 seeks to establish a form of national health care, by shifting costs to employers rather than to the public.

Reasons for Rejecting New Federal Mandate

1. It places new burdens on the free enterprise system which will result in increased costs to employers. The cost to provide and fund benefits for the uninsured will be passed on to the employer in the form of: (a) increased administrative cost; (b) poor plan experience causing increased cost to *all* participants; and (c) adverse selection against the plans.
2. It would favor interest groups, especially those who represent the provider sector of the health care industry. For the past several years, health care costs have continued to rise and treatment of conditions in many situations may have gone far beyond what is required. Providers have long capitalized on funding their services through group health care arrangements. The medicare program is living proof of what a blank check can do to any provider. This will surely exacerbate the problem of rising costs.

H. Clay Bennett

". . . We've started practicing preventive health care . . . our income prevents any . . ."

3. It mandates that employers must continue their group health plan for employees who terminate regardless of the reason for termination and their dependents. Employer sponsored plans are designed to cover the active work force, not those who elect to leave the company or are laid off. In fact most group plans already contain provisions for such occurrences and in many cases provide the right to convert to individual plans. However, such rights are not granted regardless of the reasons for termination. To mandate that employers *must* continue coverage for employees who terminate and, at the cost of the employer, will undermine the employer-employee relationship and will create a further incentive for many employers to drop their employer sponsored benefit plans. Should this occur, an even greater "uninsured" problem will be created.

4. The provision for a special open enrollment would have a devastating effect on group plans. S. 2403 provides the opportunity for employed spouses of laid off workers to

"select" against the group plan which will result in higher benefits, resulting in adverse experience requiring substantial rate adjustment to the employer sponsored plan. This is unfair cost shifting.

5. S. 2403 also requires all states to establish "pools" to cover *all* people who do not have health insurance, even if they elected not to purchase coverage on their own. Yet, many states already have in place some form of social aid and state residents as well as business are already helping to fund these state programs. S. 2403 will only serve to complicate matters and make "health care abuse" an even more attractive activity than it already is.

On the positive side, S. 2403 would create a new incentive for small business to provide benefits to all employees as well as the owners of sole proprietorships, partnerships and sub-chapter corporations. Under this provision, employers will be able to deduct their personal premium provided they extend the offer to include their employees under the plan. This provision we can support.

In conclusion, S. 2403 does not solve the problem of providing coverage to uninsureds. It would only place further burdens on the private system and will encourage greater abuses in the health care provider sector. Inevitably reduction in the protection afforded by private health plans will place new burdens on already over utilized government programs. We urge you to reject S. 2403 and to continue present broad tax incentives for American business to continue to provide effective employer sponsored health care plans without mandating the content and scope of these plans.

HEALTH CARE ALTERNATIVES FOR THE POOR

A PUBLIC HEALTH CARE FINANCING SYSTEM

Bert Seidman

Bert Seidman is director of the Department of Occupational Safety, Health, and Social Security of the American Federation of Labor and Congress of Industrial Organizations (AFL-CIO).

Points to Consider

1. How is the population of inadequately insured Americans made up?
2. What dubious distinctions does the United States enjoy among advanced industrial nations when it comes to the provision of health care?
3. Why are general hospitals being threatened as "providers of last resort" with regard to uncompensated care?
4. What are the AFL-CIO's main concerns about state risk pools?

Excerpted from testimony before the Intergovernmental Relations Subcommittee of the Senate Government Affairs Committee on Access to Health Care Services, June 26, 1986.

Only in the United States are individuals with chronic health care problems locked out of the system because they cannot obtain insurance protection.

The AFL-CIO is pleased to present testimony today in support of S. 2403, the Improved Access to Health Care Initiative. We in organized labor share the committee's concern about the dramatic growth over the past five years in the number of citizens without health insurance protection and, thus, without regular access to the health care delivery system. A less obvious problem, but with equally serious ramifications for policy makers, is the shocking jump in the number of individuals who are judged to have inadequate health insurance coverage. A recent study by the Washington, D.C. Government Research Corporation estimated this population to be as large as 50 million. Adding this to the 35 million known to be without any health care protection, two-thirds of whom are in the workforce or their dependents, there is a total universe of 85 million people who do not have adequate access to health care services.

A National System

The AFL-CIO strongly believes that the best medicine for this problem would be the enactment of a national health care system, which makes access to basic health care services a right for all Americans. Of all the industrialized countries except South Africa, only in the United States is health care coverage tied to one's job or other source of income and the decision whether to provide coverage left to an individual's employer. Only in the United States are individuals with chronic health care problems locked out of the system because they cannot obtain insurance protection. And only in the United States are children of the working poor and retirees who are not yet eligible for Medicare denied early treatment for potentially serious medical conditions because of a lack of protection and an inability to pay for health care services.

Insurance

The problem of the uninsured and underinsured has escalated as a result of a confluence of public and private sector events.

Vital Statistics

In vital statistics such as infant mortality and life expectancy, many other advanced industrial countries have better records, and the comparative situation is deteriorating. To take one well-advertised trend, infant mortality in the U.S., which in 1965 was 24.7 per 1,000 fell between that year and 1982 at a rate of 4.4% a year till in 1982 it stood at 11.5 per 1,000. The rate of decline in 1983 was only 2.6% and provisional data for 1984 show a rate of decline of 2.8%, giving a rate of 10.9 per 1,000. This compares with a rate of 8 per 1,000 in Denmark and 8.1 in Norway.

Almost all industrialized countries have some kind of universal health coverage. Not the U.S., where a patchwork quilt of programs offers protection to some. But by 1984, 38 million people, nearly 20% of the population, were without any form of private or public insurance coverage—in both absolute and percentage terms, more uncovered people than in any other developed Western society. Furthermore, 100 million Americans do not have catastrophic insurance coverage (a lack to which the president has addressed himself). Unsurprisingly, inability to pay the doctor's or the hospital's bill is one of the leading causes of personal bankruptcy.

Alexander Cockburn, *Wall Street Journal*, February 13, 1986

There have been cutbacks in public programs to the point where Medicaid now covers less than 50 percent of those living under the poverty line. Because of excessive increases in the cost of insurance, purchasers in the private sector have become more "price sensitive" and increasingly unwilling to subsidize the cost of care to the uninsured, which now amounts to approximately $6 billion nationally and threatens the very existence of public hospitals and "providers of last resort" for those without coverage or with inadequate protection.

Legislation

We commend you, Mr. Chairman, and the other sponsors of S. 2403 for introducing legislation which could help to provide much needed health care protection for those who are currently uncovered. However, we do have a number of concerns about the bill.

First, S. 2403 will address the short-term health care needs of the unemployed who, when laid off, not only experience the trauma of joblessness but also lose their link to the health care system. Although we view the requirement that employers continue coverage for four months after layoff as a positive step, it will not address the needs of the 25 percent of the unemployed who have been jobless for more than 4 months. Conceivably these individuals might have a higher probability of obtaining treatment with the enactment of the bill's requirement that states establish a mechanism to provide funding to hospitals to offset bad debt and charity care. However, a study published in the May 1, 1986 edition of the *New England Journal of Medicine* demonstrates what many health policy analysts have known for some time: that health care indirectly funded in this manner is far less adequate than services provided under public programs, such as Medicaid.

Second, we are concerned that, absent any targeting requirements in the bill for state insurance pools, public hospitals and other facilities serving a disproportionate share of patients without insurance protection may not receive their "fair share" of funds. We believe that the federal legislation should require states to give priority to these institutions and encourage hospitals to provide outpatient care when appropriate.

Third, although the bill attempts to limit what constitutes bad debt and charity care by specifying what would not be reimbursable under this section, it neglects to mention shortfalls as a result of hospital discounts given to large non-governmental payors. We believe that such a provision should be added to bar facilities from shifting the costs of such discounts on to state uncompensated care pools.

Fourth, we believe that somewhere in the bill a definition of "bad debt and charity care" and "underinsured" ought to be spelled out.

Fifth, if Congress intends to allow states to deal with the uninsured and underinsured problem by allowing them to set up a managed system of care, then it should specify what it means by managed care, in addition to requiring some basic quality controls to protect the health of potential participants.

Risk Pools

With respect to the issue of requiring employers to contribute to a state pool for individuals who cannot obtain insurance protection because they are chronically ill or at high risk of becoming ill, the AFL-CIO supports the principle underlying this provision that there should be an equitable risk-sharing arrangement to distribute the cost of care for victims of chronic diseases. We have long held that individuals and their employers should not be unfairly penalized for poor health status and would view the enactment of this provision as a positive step forward. Although some states are now considering establishing such a pool, only nine have actually done so.

On the other hand, although the bill sets a maximum on premiums that can be charged to individuals participating in state risk pools, this cap will no doubt become the only rate, leaving us with serious concerns about the potential pool of eligibles who will not be able to afford such coverage. Both the premium and out-of-pocket maximums, which also are certain to become the exclusive amounts may be affordable only to families with relatively high incomes. In the interest of equity, we believe that the committee should consider instructing states to establish a sliding scale based on income for premium requirements, as well as out-of-pocket payments. Currently, the bill would merely not prohibit a state from doing so. In addition, it should be clearly spelled out in the bill that a state may not charge higher rates to those individuals with relatively poor medical histories.

Before concluding our statement, Mr. Chairman, the AFL-CIO would like to inform the Committee that it has been working with a group of its affiliated unions and consumer organizations to develop a model initiative of our own to address the needs of the uninsured and underinsured. Our model, which will be available shortly, has a federal and state component. Like S. 2403, it would offer states various options for improving access to care. However, we recommend requiring states to establish a public commission, with a majority of its members, health care consumers, to implement such a plan. It would also require that hospitals with the greatest need be targeted for relief from expenditures for bad debt and charity care, and it would set out general guidelines for case management systems and it would require hospitals that receive funds to establish systems by which outpatient care can be provided to patients in situations where inpatient care is not warranted. In addition to the federal component, we are preparing a model state bill that would take the next step and implement the federal guidelines. At the appropriate time we would be pleased to share this model with the Subcommittee and staff.

HEALTH CARE
ALTERNATIVES FOR
THE POOR

A PRIVATE HEALTH CARE
FINANCING SYSTEM

U.S. Chamber of Commerce

The following statement was made by Robert E. Petricelli, chairman of the U.S. Chamber of Commerce's Health Care Council and president of the Affiliated Businesses Group of CIGNA Corporation.

Points to Consider

1. What are the successes claimed for the private health care financing system by the U.S. Chamber of Commerce?
2. Why does the Chamber oppose benefit mandates in the proposed legislation?
3. What will some employers feel compelled to do when faced with these mandates?
4. How does the Chamber feel about uncompensated care plans being enacted by the states?

Excerpted from testimony before the Subcommittee on Intergovernmental Relations of the Senate Committee on Government Affairs, June 26, 1986, titled *Access to Health Insurance and Health Care.*

The Chamber supports the present system of voluntary, nondiscriminatory, private-sector health-care benefit plans that vary in accordance with the needs and preferences of the workforce.

On behalf of the U.S. Chamber of Commerce, I appreciate the opportunity to comment on various provisions of S. 2403, "The Access to Health Care Act of 1986." The Chamber shares the Senate's interest in improving access to health care and addressing serious gaps in coverage. Toward this end, the Chamber's Health Care Council has established task forces on uncompensated care and retiree health care, two areas of public concern. We are in the process of assessing various options and look forward to working with the members of Congress in developing public policies that address these concerns.

Private Health-Care

Before addressing specific provisions of the proposed legislations, I want particularly to acknowledge the scope and success of the voluntary private health-care financing system that has evolved over the past two decades. Most Americans under age 65 are covered by one or more forms of private health benefits. Eighty-five percent are covered by employer-sponsored health insurance. Employers currently spend an estimated $100 billion each year on health-care benefits. As a percentage of wages and salaries, group health insurance expenditures have increased over fivefold since 1960.

The Chamber supports the present system of voluntary, nondiscriminatory, private-sector health-care benefit plans that vary in accordance with the needs and preferences of the workforce. Health-care benefits are a valuable protection for workers and their families. Employment-based group coverage is the most efficient and cost-effective means for financing health care. Clearly, the federal government has been instrumental in promoting the growth and success of this private-sector approach, primarily through tax incentives, without dictating the terms of these plans . . .

Socialist Ideas

Any discussion of economics in medical care is emotionally charged, because people naturally fear sickness, dependency, and death. Their fear may be exploited to cloud their powers or reasoning, making health care an excellent hook for introducing socialist ideas.

Jane M. Orient, M.D. *The Freeman,* June, 1982

Tax Incentives for the Self-Employed

The proposed legislation, which would extend a business tax deduction for health care purchased by unincorporated businesses—which are virtually all small businesses—and the self-employed, builds on the strengths of the voluntary system. It treats small businesses and the self-employed more equitably and will result in the increased availability of health-care coverage for their employees. The Chamber endorses this targeted extension of tax benefits.

The Chamber is pleased that the Senate version of the Tax Reform Act, H.R. 3838, also allows for a tax deduction for the self-employed and has urged members of the Committee on Ways and Means to support that aspect of the Senate tax measure when it is considered in conference.

Extension of Health Coverage for Former Workers

In contrast to positive incentives, the proposed legislation pursues a federal benefit mandate strategy, specifically targeted in this instance to extend coverage for laid-off workers, at the employer's expense. The Chamber traditionally has opposed and continues to oppose state and federal government requirements that mandate plan design.

There are sound reasons for this opposition. Employers face an increasingly complex and costly array of benefit mandates. The number of state mandated benefit laws has increased from fewer than 50 in 1974 to over 600 in 1985. State mandates encompass a host of provider groups and various treatment categories in addition to continuation and conversion requirements. In some instances, the states mandate coverage; in other instances, the states require that the coverage be made available at the employer's option. In all instances, self-insured plans are exempt under the Employee Retirement Income Security Act (ERISA) . . .

The proposed federal mandate to extend coverage to former employees for four months at the employer's expense closely follows the Consolidated Omnibus Reconciliation Act of 1985 (COBRA) continuation of coverage mandate. The COBRA provisions require employers to continue to make available health-care plans to various categories of former employees and family members (at the individual's expense) for periods ranging from 18 to 36 months. Imposition of federal mandates on the existing state requirements has created inordinate confusion. Enactment of additional federal mandates at this time only will compound implementation and compliance problems.

Mandated extension of coverage for laid-off workers would impose additional health benefit costs on businesses when they are least able to afford the extra burden. The adverse economic impact of such a counter-cyclical * proposal requires scrutiny . . .

Employers Feel the Pinch

The Chamber's *1984 Employee Benefits Survey* indicates that employers dedicate nearly 37 percent of compensation costs to employee benefits. This includes legally required, as well as voluntarily provided, benefits. International competition is forcing many firms to assess labor costs and consider available mechanisms for reducing production costs. Certain health benefit mandates simply increase labor costs, force employers to consider benefit trade-offs, and reduce the employer's ability to meet the real needs of the employees. In some instances, if employers are faced with the prospect of health-care expenses for former employees, they will offer either less generous health plans or higher copayments and deductibles or, in the extreme,

---

* Counter-cyclical: Burdens on employers would increase when economy is doing poorly.

offer no health-care coverage. Alternatively, employers may offer fewer other benefits to terminated employees, such as severance benefits or job relocation or retraining services. Other employee benefits for all workers may be curtailed in order to keep overall compensation costs affordable.

Priorities Must Be Set

Fiscal realities, in both public and private sectors, compel us to set priorities even among socially desirable goals. We propose that serious consideration be given to direct benefit costs and indirect economic effects of pursuing additional mandated benefits. In effect, economic-impact analysis will permit the weighing of competing public policy objectives prior to enactment of legislation. The Chamber stands ready to assist in gathering and analyzing the data needed to study this matter . . .

Risk Pools for the Medically Uninsurable

The Chamber has not taken a formal position on the establishment of state risk pools for medically uninsurable individuals. Clearly, health coverage for this population is an important goal. Among the comments during Chamber Health Care Council discussion of this proposal is the acknowledgement that risk pools can ameliorate a part of the uninsured health-care problem. However, a number of Chamber members have raised concerns that legislation that requires those employers offering health care coverage to their employees to fund any financial shortfall in the risk pool is potentially costly and is a disincentive to offer health care-insurance. These matters require further study by the Chamber and, we believe, by the Congress, as well.

State Insurance and Uncompensated-Care Plans

The Chamber shares the Subcommittee's concern about uncompensated care. We are concerned, however, by the bill's open-ended proposal that directs states to establish insurance programs for the uninsured and underinsured. A number of states are experimenting with various hospital uncompensated-care financing mechanisms. Ongoing state programs may offer models for other states. Any solutions adopted in this area, however, must not discourage attention to hospital care costs or continued underfunding of costs by Medicaid and Medicare. At this time, federally mandating state insurance plans, especially in such a sweeping fashion, is quite premature.

In conclusion, the Chamber and I stand ready to work with this Subcommittee in support of legislative provisions that will increase both the availability and affordability of private health insurance coverage consistent with other economic pressures facing employers. Also, we would welcome the opportunity to explore in greater detail our proposal for closer economic and policy analysis of mandated benefits as a means for avoiding the myriad of problems posed by such a mandated benefits strategy.

HEALTH CARE ALTERNATIVES FOR THE POOR

A MULTI-FACETED FINANCING SYSTEM

Jack W. Owen

Jack W. Owen is Executive Vice President of the American Hospital Association.

Points to Consider

1. Why is Medicaid increasingly less able to meet the insurance needs of the indigent?
2. Does Medicare or Medicaid provide any subsidies to hospitals for indigent care?
3. How would the AHA reform Medicaid?

Excerpted from testimony by Jack W. Owen before the Senate Subcommittee on Intergovernmental Relations of the Committee on Governmental Affairs, June 26, 1986.

*Medical indigence is a complex, multi-faceted issue
that has no single, or simple, solution.*

The highest priority for our Association, which represents
5,600 institutional and 40,000 personal members, is finding a
solution to the growing crisis of medical indigence. In February
of 1985 the AHA Board's Special Committee on Care for the
Indigent completed its report, *Cost and Compassion: Recommendations for Avoiding a Crisis in Care for the Medically Indigent,*
which outlines a series of long- and short-term public and private
initiatives which could be adopted to address the problem. Many
of the approaches we recommended are also proposed in the
Access to Health Care Act of 1986. For this reason, we applaud
the sponsors' efforts, we consider the proposed bills an important
first step toward solving the problem, and we welcome the
opportunity to present our views on this high-priority issue.

Twenty years after the creation of Medicaid, medical indigence is again becoming a major problem for a large and
increasing number of Americans, and therefore a major policy
issue for federal, state, and local government, providers, and
consumers of health care services. A sizable percentage of the
population is unable to obtain private insurance and does not
qualify for public insurance programs. The persistence of a large
population without adequate health insurance coverage imposes
large costs on all members of society.

In February 1985, the Board of Trustees of the American
Hospital Association established a Special Committee on Care
for the Indigent to document the nature and magnitude of the
indigent care problem, and to recommend AHA policy initiatives
to address this issue at the local, state, and national levels. The
committee undertook a comprehensive review and analysis of the
causes, manifestations, and consequences of the problem and
recommended a variety of long- and short-term actions that
government, businesses, insurers, and providers could take to
solve it. The final report of the special committee, *Cost and
Compassion: Recommendations for Avoiding a Crisis in Care for
the Medically Indigent,* was accepted by the Board at its February
1986 annual meeting, and will be sent to members of this
committee upon its publication in July.

The report shows a problem of startling and growing
dimensions:

Double the National Rate

In 1984, Washington D.C. recorded 21.2 infant deaths for 1,000 live births. That was almost double the national rate of 10.8 infant deaths per 1,000 live births and higher than the rate for countries like Cuba, with 19, and Costa Rica, with 19.

For blacks in Washington, the rate was even higher—24.3 in 1984.

Associated Press, March, 1987

- *The size and characteristics of the uninsured.* In 1983, nearly 33 million Americans were without private health insurance or were not covered by governmental health benefit programs. Nearly two-thirds of the uninsured were employed or were members of families in which the head of the household was employed and often insured. However, the jobs held by the uninsured are frequently marginal. Two-thirds of the uninsured have family incomes less than twice the federal poverty level and one-third fall below the federal poverty guidelines. These characteristics have an important bearing on the extent to which private insurance can resolve the problem of medical indigence.
- *The inadequacy of Medicaid.* Although Medicaid is often thought to be the principal means of financing care for the indigent, it now covers less than 40 percent of the poor. Medicaid must now be viewed principally as a program of supplementary coverage for the aged (nursing home care) and disabled medically indigent who are eligible for and receive benefits under Medicare.

In 1984, barely one-fourth of Medicaid's expenditures paid for care needed by the non-Medicare eligible poor. Three-quarters of Medicaid's expenditures paid for services provided to individuals already covered by Medicare: primary care and other acute care services not covered by Medicare; extended long-term care for Medicare beneficiaries (nursing home care); and Medicare Part B premiums (non-hospital insurance).

● *Rapid growth of unsponsored care.* At the same time that Medicaid has been providing coverage for a declining percentage of the poor, the amount of uncompensated care provided by hospitals has risen sharply. State and local government tax appropriations have not kept pace with the growth in uncompensated care. Unsponsored care—the care that must be subsidized by the private sector—more than doubled between 1980 and 1984. In 1984 unsponsored care amounted to $5.7 billion or 4.6 percent of total hospital expenses, up from 3.6 percent of total expenses in 1980.

● *Declining sources of private subsidy.* Traditionally, hospitals have been compelled—and have been able—to subsidize the cost of care provided to the medically indigent by increasing charges to privately insured patients and patients able to pay their own bills. Between 1980 and 1984, the ability of hospitals to subsidize non-paying patients declined sharply. The principal sources of government financing, Medicare and Medicaid, provide no subsidies for the costs of indigent care. As competitive pressures on private insurers and providers increase, private sources of funds will continue to diminish.

The committee concluded that these trends threaten to limit access to care by the poor and therefore jeopardize the viability of the competitive approach to health care. In an increasingly competitive industry, those hospitals serving substantial numbers of the indigent will be unable to survive without explicit public support. If a method of financing care for the medically indigent within a competitive system cannot be found, pressures to return to more regulatory methods may be irresistible. The special AHA committee on care for the indigent recommended a variety of long-and short-term measures to avert this crisis.

Solving the Indigent Care Problem:
Long-Term Approaches

Medical indigence is a complex, multi-faceted issue that has no single, or simple, solution. Because the public expects needed care to be provided regardless of a patient's ability to pay, all members of society must participate in the financing of care provided to the medically indigent. This public responsibility does not mean, however, that government alone can or will resolve the problem. An enduring solution to the problem of medical

'HMMM – UM HMMM'

Reprinted by permission of the *St. Louis Globe-Democrat*.

indigence will require initiatives by both the public and private sectors to:

● reduce the size of the medically indigent population through adequate private health insurance; and

● restructure and extend public programs to finance care for the medically indigent who are unable to obtain private insurance.

Private insurance can be made more widely available through the cooperative efforts of federal, state, and local government, private insurers, employers, and providers. However, as competition increases and resources become more constrained, a residual public program is essential to finance care for those who cannot obtain private health insurance. To strengthen the public financing of care for the medically indigent, several actions should be pursued:

● The reorganization of Medicaid into three distinct programs: a program of acute care coverage for the medically indigent who are not eligible for Medicare; a program of supplementary acute care coverage for Medicare beneficiaries; and a program of long-term care coverage for Medicare beneficiaries.

● The gradual strengthening of the federal role in funding Medicaid: a trust fund sponsored by a broadly based tax, for example a payroll tax. Such a tax could provide a stable source of funding for Medicaid, would equitably distribute the cost of the program, and properly structured, could create a positive incentive for employers and employees to obtain private health insurance.

● Reform of delivery and payment systems: the adoption of innovative payment and delivery arrangements would encourage the efficient use and production of the health care services needed by individuals enrolled in Medicaid.

Averting the Indigent Care Crisis: Short-Term Initiatives

Although the elements of a long-term solution to the problem of medical indigence can be readily identified, adoption and implementation of a comprehensive solution will take time. It is essential that there be no deterioration of existing programs during these deliberations. Moreover, while the debate over the long-term solution proceeds, the issue should be dealt with through a series of incremental steps that strengthen incentives to provide employer-paid health insurance and that gradually strengthen public programs . . .

Alternatives to Improve Public and Private Funding

Under no circumstances should the federal government reduce the level of federal funding available to state Medicaid programs, nor should it mandate or allow states to reduce entitlement under Medicaid. In addition,

- The expansion of Medicaid eligibility should be accomplished as federal resources permit, with the objective of achieving a uniform standard of eligibility under state Medicaid programs by 1990.
- The federal government should phase in the long-term reforms in Medicaid described above, including the creation of a stable, dedicated source of funding.
- To encourage provider participation in Medicaid and to eliminate the need for private-sector subsidies of Medicaid expenditures, Medicare and Medicaid payment levels generally should be comparable to those for private patients, that is, the ratio of payments to costs should be approximately the same for public and private payers, although the methods of payment may be different.

States should maintain eligibility and funding levels for Medicaid and other programs designed to finance care for the indigent. As their resources permit, states should expand Medicaid coverage to include both the medically needy and other segments of the medically indigent population.

States should establish risks pools for high-risk or uninsurable individuals. All insurers should participate in such risk pools, including Blue Cross plans, commercial insurers, and self-insured businesses. The federal government should facilitate this by modifying the exemption of self-insured employers from state laws regulating the business of insurance.

Local government should maintain or increase funding for public or other government-supported providers. Within metropolitan regions, governments should identify methods of expanding the population base responsible for funding public providers. Local government should also evaluate the possible benefits of adopting formally organized systems for delivery of care.

Employers and insurers should work with government to ensure adequate funding for the medically indigent who must rely on public support. If adequate public funding is not made available, employers should work with providers and insurers to establish funding mechanisms for care provided to the medically indigent.

Hospitals should maintain their historical commitment to provide care to those who need care, including the indigent; should take appropriate actions to raise public awareness of the implications of purchaser actions on the ability of the hospital to care for the medically indigent; and should work with employers, insurers, and government to develop viable short- and long-term solutions to the problem of medical indigence.

HEALTH CARE
ALTERNATIVES FOR
THE POOR

HEALTH CARE OPTIONS FOR THE
WORKING POOR

Leonard Inskip

Leonard Inskip is an associate editor of the Minneapolis Star and Tribune.

Points to Consider

1. What are the services provided by the Metro Community Health Consortium clinics?
2. Why has this consortium been successful?
3. How do the clinics set their fees?
4. How does the consortium solve its staffing problems?

Leonard Inskip, "Consortium Helps Deliver Health Care to Working Poor," *Minneapolis Star and Tribune,* November 23, 1983. Reprinted with permission of the Minneapolis Star and Tribune.

"We still run into people who think everyone in the United States has health care guaranteed." That's not true for the working poor, who represent "a gap in the health-care system."

When New Jersey's governor and top business leaders visited Minnesota recently to learn about public/private partnerships, one of the groups on their program was the Metro Community Health Consortium.

The consortium, whose name is hardly a household phrase, serves an important public function: medical care for the working poor. These are people whose income or assets are enough to deny them government-financed medical care, but who are too poor to afford unsubsidized care.

This year, more than 30,000 working poor will get low-cost medical or dental care from the consortium's 12 neighborhood or community clinics in the Twin Cities. The clinics also provide education to prevent sickness.

Preventive Care

The clinics, mostly located in low-income neighborhoods, were set up in the late 1960s and early 1970s. Volunteers started them, often in storefronts. One goal was to emphasize preventive care rather than merely treating sickness after the fact. Another was to give neighborhoods and lay people greater control over medical care. In the mid-1970s, the clinics began getting government help; that led to creation of the consortium as a means to improve the clinics' effectiveness, including record-keeping for government grants.

The clinics were part of a national wave. In other cities, many failed. But all survived in the Twin Cities, says Margy Weber, the consortium's development director.

A reason for success here has been the consortium, which provides assistance in management, fundraising, technical services, record-keeping, billing, quality standards and training. Also important are support from government, business and foundations, plus the work of hundreds of volunteers (students to doctors) from the health-care field.

116

37 Million

The American economy is shifting jobs from union-ized industries to unorganized service companies. The Administration has tightened welfare and Medicaid eligibility. And the number of Americans unable to afford medical care has grown in just five years from 25 million to 37 million.

Hospitals and clinics once got away with padding other patients' bills to raise the $6 billion a year it costs to care for the uninsured. Now, Federal and private insurance plans are tightening up on reimbursements and eliminating this hidden subsidy. As a result, according to a recent study by the Robert Wood Johnson Foundation, a million Americans each year are now refused medical treatment and five million others don't even seek help they need.

Editorial, *New York Times,* May 30, 1987

Low Paying Jobs

An estimated 200,000 working poor live in the metropolitan area, Weber says. Forty percent of the patients are at or below federal poverty levels, but only 13 percent qualify for government-paid medical assistance. The average family of four served by the clinics has an income of $12,224, compared with a poverty guideline of $9,900 for the same-size family and an average income of $27,931 for the metropolitan area. Only half the patients have any health insurance, and only one-quarter or less have insurance that covers even part of clinic bills.

Typically, clients have low-paying jobs in small businesses without insurance programs. Or they are self-employed, un-deremployed, seasonally employed or unemployed.

"We still run into people," Weber says, "who think everyone in the United States has health care guaranteed." That's not true, she says, for the working poor, who represent "a gap in the health-care system."

117

The clinics and the coalition attempt to fill that gap. When the clinics started, they were free. But volunteer services were limited, and clinics often were open only a few hours weekly. Now the clinics have paid staffs supplemented by volunteers. They charge sliding-scale fees based on patients' income. Collectively, the clinics had cash revenues of $3.7 million last year and noncash donations of goods and services worth $470,000. The clinics had 67,000 patient visits for medical care, 10,000 for dental care and 64,000 for education, support groups and counseling.

Last year, the consortium raised about $300,000 from a blue-chip group of corporations and foundations. The consortium sponsors a federated fund drive for nine of the clinics. Also last year, it administered $265,000 in federal and state funds allocated to clinics by the city of Minneapolis. The coalition's own budget was just over $100,000 for its programs and a staff of three full-time and two part-time people. In all, the clinics got about $1.9 million from government sources in 1982, $570,000 from private sources and nearly $1.2 million from patients, insurance programs or welfare.

Cooperation

The 12 clinics (eight in Minneapolis, two in suburbs and two in St. Paul) are moving toward closer cooperation. With financial help from the St. Paul Companies, the coalition this year began a pilot project in which two professional employees serve more than one clinic. Previously, when a doctor or a nurse practitioner took a vacation, a clinic might have had to suspend or severely reduce certain activities; many have only one doctor. The coalition this year added a half-time substitute doctor and a half-time substitute nurse who will fill in at clinics when needed. If this system—patterned after teacher substitutes in schools —works, the coalition may add a shared medical technologist, dentist and pharmacist.

The same St. Paul Companies grant is being used to develop a program of volunteer substitutes for volunteers who on short notice find they can't meet their volunteer schedule—say, a doctor detained at a hospital.

A Network

Perhaps most interesting, the grant is helping build a network of medical specialists who will charge the working poor the same

"GIVE IT TO ME STRAIGHT, DOC — HOW MUCH TIME HAVE I GOT TO RAISE MONEY FOR THE HOSPITAL BILL?"

©1979 HERBLOCK

Copyright 1979 by Herblock in the *Washington Post*.

sliding scale used by the clinic that refers them. Clinic doctors found that anywhere between 50 and 90 percent of their patients were not following up on referrals because patients couldn't afford specialists' fees. With the help of the Hennepin and Ramsey medical associations, the coalition has signed up 211 specialists. "The response is wonderful," Weber says. The sliding scale ranges from zero to 100 percent.

Services Vary

The coalition, whose offices are in St. Paul, is looking at the feasibility of a prepaid health plan for the working poor. Such a plan also would involve a sliding scale.

All the clinics provide primary medical care. Some provide dental work. One has optometry. But services may vary, and each clinic reflects the wishes of its board, drawn mainly from its neighborhood. The local base has been a strength of the clinics, Weber says.

On Dec. 2, the consortium will mark its 10th anniversary by holding a fundraising buffet—the first joint fundraising event by the clinics. Appropriately, the event will be on the West Bank at the Cedar Riverside People's Center—where the metropolitan area's first community clinic began in 1969. That clinic is still there.

WHAT IS EDITORIAL BIAS?

This activity may be used as an individualized study guide for students in libraries and resource centers or as a discussion catalyst in small group and classroom discussions.

The capacity to recognize an author's point of view is an essential reading skill. The skill to read with insight and understanding involves the ability to detect different kinds of opinions or bias. Sex bias, race bias, ethnocentric bias, political bias and religious bias are five basic kinds of opinions expressed in editorials and all literature that attempts to persuade. They are briefly defined below.

5 KINDS OF EDITORIAL BIAS

sex bias— the expression of dislike for and/or feeling of superiority over the opposite sex or a particular sexual minority

race bias—the expression of dislike for and/or feeling of superiority over a racial group

ethnocentric bias—the expression of a belief that one's own group, race, religion, culture or nation is superior. Ethnocentric persons judge others by their own standards and values.

political bias—the expression of political opinions and attitudes about domestic or foreign affairs

religious bias—the expression of a religious belief or attitude

Guidelines

1. From the readings in chapter three, locate five sentences that provide examples of editorial opinion or bias.

2. Write down each of the above sentences and determine what kind of bias each sentence represents. Is it sex bias, race bias, ethnocentric bias, political bias or religious bias?
3. Make up one sentence statements that would be an example of each of the following: *sex bias, race bias, ethnocentric bias, political bias* and *religious bias?*
4. See if you can locate five sentences that are factual statements from the readings in chapter three.

CHAPTER 4

PRIVATIZING HEALTH CARE FOR THE POOR

15 PRIVATIZING HEALTH CARE FOR THE POOR

FOR-PROFIT HOSPITALS MAKING HEALTH CARE WORSE

Peter Downs

Peter Downs is a free-lance writer in St. Charles, Missouri. Research for this article was assisted by a grant from the Fund for Investigative Journalism.

Points to Consider

1. What does the case of Joe Allen Bennett demonstrate?
2. How common has patient dumping become?
3. What are some of the yearly remunerations for top corporate health officers?
4. Why are profits soaring for non-profit hospitals?

Peter Downs, "Your Money or Your Life," *The Progressive,* January, 1987, pages 24–8. Copyright © 1987, The Progressive, Inc. Reprinted by permission from the Progressive, Madison, WI 53703.

With the for-profit companies in the vanguard, hospitals around the country are refusing treatment to the indigent.

Joe Allen Bennett lived on a fourteen-acre farm in College Grove, Tennessee, with his disabled wife. They had a combined income of $328 in 1983, and they had no health insurance.

Bennett suffered from lung cancer. After an emergency biopsy revealed his condition in October 1983, he was referred to the Park View Hospital in Nashville. Park View, owned by the Hospital Corporation of America (HCA), was one of the few facilities in the area that provided the radiology treatment he needed.

When Bennett and his sister, Mattie Sue Owens, arrived at Park View, they were told that no treatment would be given until $500 had been paid. He did not have the $500. Neither did his sister. The most they could come up with was $300. That wasn't enough.

Distressed, they talked with HCA vice president John Colton. "HCA does not provide care to anyone without assurance of payment," Colton told them.

Bennett's family struggled to scrape together $500 so he could begin treatment. A few days later, however, HCA upped the ante: Unless Bennett paid another $500, the treatment would be stopped.

By then Bennett was in great pain and coughing up large amounts of blood. His family approached Legal Services attorney Gordon Bonnyman for help. Bonnyman contacted HCA's counsel, who said the corporation "turned down people in similar circumstances every day" and would make no exception in Bennett's case.

Bonnyman threatened legal action. On the day he was going to file a complaint charging the company with abandonment, denial of emergency care, intentional infliction of mental distress, and extortion, HCA finally agreed to continue treatment. Bennett died of lung cancer in June 1984.

Dumping the Indigent

What happened at Park View is not unique. With the for-profit companies in the vanguard, hospitals around the country are refusing treatment to the indigent.

Hospitals in the United States fall into three categories: for-profit hospitals, which are in business to make money for their investors; not-for-profit hospitals, which nonetheless can earn profits, and public hospitals, which are owned by the Federal, state, or local government.

HCA, the largest for-profit hospital company, owns 230 general and psychiatric hospitals in the United States, and it manages another 196. Almost all of its facilities are in the South, half of them in Florida, Tennessee, and Texas.

Four of HCA's five Nashville hospitals provided no charity care in 1980. One year later, they gave $1.8 million in such care, compared to the $30 million provided by the city's eight not-for-profit hospitals. For-profit hospitals in Tennessee routinely gave no charity care in 1984, dumping the indigent onto public facilities.

Hard-Nosed Attitude

The officers of HCA have a reason for their hard-nosed attitude. Generous bonus plans tie their own income to company profitability. From 1983 through 1985, Thomas Frisk Jr., chairman and chief executive officer of HCA, received salary and benefits totaling $4.9 million. The top eighteen HCA officers were paid $35 million during those years, and the company retained earnings of $878 million.

HCA makes money for its owners and officers by "discounts in the purchases of medical and dietary supplies and capital equipment due to our favorably priced national purchasing contracts, reductions in patient bad debts, carefully selected decreases in staffing levels, and reductions in inventory levels," its 1985 annual report states.

What's more, HCA is growing fat on taxpayer money. Approximately 44 per cent of the company's revenues come from Medicare and Medicaid. It is skimming the Government even as it skimps the public.

But HCA is not alone. The Humana Corporation, one of the top four hospital giants, operates the same way. In 1983, the Kentucky attorney general's office ordered Humana's Lake Cumberland Hospital in Somerset, Kentucky, to stop holding patients hostage. Hospital officials had told parents they could not take their newborns home until they had paid their bills. Other

Profit Motive

The profit motive is detrimental to health care for the basic reason that profit, not meeting human needs, becomes the overriding purpose of the hospital. Thus the quality of health care is sacrificed to the extent that it stands in the way of the goal of maximizing profits and for-profits hospitals can only make a bad situation worse.

Editorial, *The People,* February 2, 1985

patients were told they could not leave the hospital until they paid $1,000 or signed a loan application.

Hospital officials agreed to stop such practices and instead began demanding pre-admission deposits. Pregnant women, for example, had to pay a deposit of $1,200 to get in the door. Women who couldn't come up with the money had to travel more than 100 miles to another facility.

"Humana hospitals do not have the responsibility to provide care for the indigent except in emergencies or in those situations where reimbursement for indigent patients is provided," the company stated on a Florida certificate-of-need application. Humana boasts that such a policy places it "in the forefront in addressing the problem of who pays for indigent care."

Salaries

Humana's chairman, David Jones, received salary and benefits totaling $2.4 million for 1983 and 1985; his compensation for 1984 reportedly topped $18 million, but that could not be confirmed with the Securities and Exchange Commission. In 1983 and 1985, Humana's top executives received $30 million in salaries and benefits, and from 1983 through 1985, the company retained earnings of $570 million.

The bonuses awarded to top Humana executives are determined by the company's earnings per share. The highest executives receive bonuses equal to 70 per cent of their base

127

pay for earnings per share of $2.25 or above. For lower earnings, the bonuses are correspondingly smaller.

Jones establishes specific performance areas to gauge his hospitals' success: bad debts (which include indigent care), staffing, overtime, accounts receivable, quality, supply expense, and pre-tax earnings. He measures quality by asking patients to assess staff courtesy and waiting time.

In 1985, each hospital in the Humana chain was to reduce the volume of bad debt by 5 per cent, unless the result would still be greater than 1983's bad debt. In such a case, the goal was to cut bad debt by 10 per cent, or to the 1983 level, whichever was higher.

Dumping Denied

Tom Nolan, a Humana public-affairs officer, acknowledges that indigent care is part of bad debt, but he claims such care is not affected by the company's bad-debt goals. "Company policy remains the same," Nolan says. "It is company policy to treat all indigent emergency cases and all indigent non-emergency cases where there is no public hospital available to provide indigent care." Humana and the other for-profits, Nolan adds, devote about the same percentage of their revenues to charity care as do the not-for-profits.

When there is both a Humana hospital and a public hospital, Humana sends indigent patients to the public hospital because that's what the public hospital gets Government money for, says Nolan, and "we pay taxes."

In 1984, the Humana hospital in Memphis provided no indigent care, while the public Regional Medical center provided $25.9 million of such care. Services provided at the for-profit hospitals are no less expensive than elsewhere; the money that used to be spent on charity care now simply goes to profit and expansion . . .

Adapting to Change

These earnings reflect the success for-profit hospitals have had in adapting to changes brought on by the Federal Government and third-party insurers. In 1984, the Government began to phase in a prospective-payment system, which reimburses hospitals at a fixed rate for each illness rather than

128

for what the hospital charges. And throughout the decade, the private health-insurance industry has been taking additional steps to restrict hospital use.

In response, the for-profit hospitals quickly moved into those areas where Federal cost controls are lax and cost pass-throughs still allowed—out-patient services, psychiatric care, new equipment, and to a lesser extent nursing homes. In addition, they began to make deals with insurance companies.

Virtually all for-profit hospitals offer discounts to insurance companies that direct patients to their facilities. American Medical International (AMI) is buying health-maintenance organizations and setting up its own insurance company, AMI-CARE, to funnel patients into its hospital system. Humana is establishing Humana Care Plus, with incentives to shuttle patients to Humana-affiliated doctors and hospitals.

Profits Soaring

In this competitive environment, the not-for-profit chains are coming to resemble the for-profits ever more closely. By pursuing cost-cutting strategies, the not-for-profit hospitals have been able to boost their profits as much as or more than the for-profit hospitals. In 1984, the profits of Catholic hospitals rose 30 per cent; other religious hospitals saw profits soar 55 per cent; secular not-for-profit hospitals enjoyed 35 per cent higher profits, while the for-profit chains boosted profits by 28 per cent.

Not-for-profit hospitals are also forming their own for-profit chains. The two biggest such ventures are Voluntary Hospitals of America (VHA) and American Healthcare Systems (AHS). VHA is owned by sixty-two large not-for-profits, including Barnes Hospital (Washington University-St. Louis), Johns Hopkins, and Yale. Its profit-making subsidiaries provide management services, hospital laundry and cleaning, psychiatric and alcoholism care, and capital development (with the Mellon Bank) to 550 community-based not-for-profit hospitals. In 1986, VHA formed a partnership with Aetna Life and Casualty called PARTNERS National Health Plans, which makes VHA hospitals the providers of choice for all Aetna-insured patients.

AHS is a partnership of thirty-five regional not-for-profit systems with 500 member hospitals. It serves its member hospitals with a mass-purchasing program and a joint venture with Transamerica Occidental and Provident Life Insurance Companies. AHS provides the network of hospitals and medical staff to serve patients in the health organizations the insurance companies market.

And, like the for-profit chains, the not-for-profits are slashing indigent care. DePaul Hospital in St. Louis, for instance, refuses to admit patients without some guarantee of payment, either from an insurance company or a patient-payment contract.

The radiation cancer therapy department of the Washington University Medical Center, also in St. Louis, is declining to take any more Medicaid patients from the city of St. Louis until the city makes up the difference between the costs to the Center and what Medicaid pays. The chief of radiation cancer therapy, Dr. Carlos Perez, says Medicaid pays only 40 per cent of the cost of the therapy.

"Even the most compassionate and committed institutions," says Senator Edward Kennedy, are being forced to choose between "rationing health care for the poor or bankruptcy for their institutions."

That's bad news for the Joe Allen Bennetts of this world.

16 PRIVATIZING HEALTH CARE FOR THE POOR

INVESTOR-OWNED HOSPITALS ARE NOT THE PROBLEM

John C. Bedrosian

John C. Bedrosian is Senior Executive Vice President of National Medical Enterprises, Incorporated. The following statement was taken from a speech made before the American Association of Hospital Planning in Chicago, Illinois.

Points to Consider

1. What justifies investor-owned hospitals being regarded as community institutions?
2. How does the for-profit hospital sector pull its weight in terms of care for the poor?
3. How can uncompensated care be provided for when a non-profit hospital is acquired?
4. Why is the growing reluctance to accept nonpaying patients not restricted to the for-profit sector?
5. How has the government reneged on its commitment to the elderly and poor?

John C. Bedrosian, in a speech delivered before the American Association for Hospital Planning, Chicago, Illinois, July 27, 1985. Reprinted by permission from *'Vital Speeches of the Day.'*

Very little difference exists between private non-profit and for-profit hospitals as to the proportion of free or otherwise uncompensated care.

According to the Robert Wood Johnson Foundation, 28 million Americans—a population greater than any single state in the Union—fall into the category of the "health care poor."

And their numbers are growing. The health care poor, and the magnitude of uncompensated services provided to them, represent a national problem demanding nothing short of a national debate.

To begin the debate on how best to deal with the problem, I have three major criticisms with my assigned topic: "Investor owned hospitals as community hospitals: can they care for rich and poor alike?"

Three Criticisms

First, for-profit hospitals *are* just as much community hospitals as non-profits are.

Second, the plight of the health care poor is *not*—as my assigned topic implies—the result of any one segment failing to do its fair share. Statistics from the American Hospital Association's annual survey show that private non-profit hospitals nationwide contribute 4.2 percent of their gross revenues to bad debt and charity care, compared to 4.4 percent for investor-owned hospitals, as reported by an annual survey of the Federation of American Hospitals. A study last year by the California Hospital Association reached a similar conclusion in the state of California: Very little difference exists between private non-profit and for-profit hospitals as to the proportion of free or otherwise uncompensated care. This should not come as a surprise.

Usually when a non-profit hospital is acquired, written into the purchase agreement is a clause that the new owner will provide an equivalent level of free care to the community. If the facility is being leased from the county, a portion of the lease payment typically goes to the provision of indigent care. And in the case of joint ventures between investor-owned and non-profit organizations, the mission of non-profit foundations—including their commitment to indigent care—remains intact.

Free Care

The more people had to pay for medical care, the less of it they used.

Free health care had no effect on bad health habits linked to heart trouble and some kinds of cancer. Even though people getting free care saw doctors once, twice or more often a year, they were just as likely to smoke, be overweight and have high blood cholesterol levels as others.

The free-care plan's effect on blood pressure, although small, could save lives among people who are at high risk because of smoking, high blood pressure and cholesterol levels. These people's risk of early death was about 10 percent lower as a result of the free care.

Daniel Q. Haney, Associated Press, December, 1983

In other words—to answer the question outright—investor-owned providers *do* approach uncompensated care in a manner and proportion consistent with non-profit hospitals. More importantly investor-owned providers contribute to uncompensated care through the payment of local property taxes, state income taxes, and federal income taxes—totaling well over half a billion dollars in 1983.

The third criticism I have with my topic is the implication that uncompensated care is simply a rich man/poor man issue, with investor-owned providers "skimming the cream." Let me use our company as an example to refute this allegation.

In fiscal year 1985 nearly 50 percent of the revenues from our 57 acute general hospitals were generated by Medicare and Medicaid patients—*not* well-to-do private pay patients; 60 percent of the revenues from our more than 300 nursing homes came from Medicare and Medicaid patients. Although Medicare is certainly not classified as "poor man's medicine," I think all of us would agree that no one is going to get rich treating the poor and the elderly at current reimbursement levels.

In addressing the issue of uncompensated care today, I want to refocus my topic to get to the heart of the issue. Uncompensated care is not an investor-owned hospital issue, and it is not a hospital issue. It is a *social* issue. The real question that needs to be asked is: Can we, *as a society,* do what is necessary to enable the health care poor to obtain access to needed health services? . .

Dumping

If the private hospitals are transferring increasing numbers of patients to public hospitals, is it not the responsibility of government to refine the very system it created which is the cause of it? I submit that the worst case of dumping taking place today is what the federal government is threatening to do to the health care industry—by reneging on promises made when Medicare prospective pricing was first conceived and approved by Congress, and by backing away from its original commitment to the poor and elderly in proposing cutbacks in both Medicare and Medicaid. This is why we have growing numbers of health care poor, many of whom are falling through the safety nets that were put in place in 1965.

The problem of government is not just at the federal level. States and counties are inadequately funding the very public hospitals they created to take care of the poor. Nationwide, the current legislative agenda at *all* levels of government is preoccupied with budget matters. As a nation, we seem to have retreated from the earlier consensus that adequate health care is the *right* of every citizen. Or, if we still consider it a right, we seem unwilling to provide the necessary resources to give the commitment meaning.

Ladies and gentlemen, I submit that our first order of business must be to halt this hasty and calculated retreat on the part of the government budget cutters. Cut out the fat and the waste, but not the heart and soul of our health care system. Before it's too late, let's challenge government to assume its proper leading role in addressing the needs of the health care poor.

Before proposing a solution, let's clarify who we are trying to help and what their needs are. It turns out that medical poverty strikes a broad cross-section of our society.

Rather than just the most destitute, we know that almost half of medical indigents come from families with annual incomes

above $15 thousand—well above the poverty level as defined by the federal government.

Rather than just minorities, almost three-fifths of medical indigents are caucasian.

Rather than just the unemployed, over half of them hold down a job all or part of the year. At least 70 percent are workers or dependents of workers.

And finally, they are relatively young: Over half are *under the age of 25* and a third are children age 18 or younger, many of them pregnant mothers and their newborns.

In other words, the health care poor represent a diverse melting pot that is boiling over because previous public policy treated the health care poor as a homogenous group. As a result, existing public and private safety nets miss the mark for millions of Americans, who are not poor enough to qualify for Medicaid, who are temporarily unemployed, or who are employed but do not have any or adequate private health coverage. In addition, our social programs miss the mark in providing the kinds of medical services the medically indigent need . . .

Pluralistic Solution

In view of the diversity of the health care poor and their various medical needs, it is unlikely that any *one* solution will be sufficient.

I would propose a *pluralistic* solution: That we *finance* the care from the broadest tax base possible; and that we *deliver* the care from the broadest provider base possible—relying not only on public hospitals, but also on primary care physicians and private community hospitals.

To finance care of the medically indigent, there must be a mechanism to tap general tax revenues, since this is a *societal* obligation. Imposing taxes on hospitals, however, is to in effect impose a tax on private patients who are hospitalized, since hospitals—like any other business —must somehow recover the additional expense through increased prices to charge-based payors. Nonetheless, individual states are trying to take matters into their own hands. An estimated 88 bills related to uncompensated care will be introduced this year by state legislatures. Some of these bills call for taxes on hospital revenues to fund care for the indigent that amount to nothing more than a "sick tax" because inevitably these taxes will find their way into the hospital rate structure . . .

Two Choices

Let's summarize the problem and solution for a moment. The problem of uncompensated care is primarily that the tax dollars paid to public hospitals to care for the indigent are not stretching far enough. And employers are less willing to cross-subsidize publicly funded and non-funded patients. With the reduction of a hospital's ability to shift costs, public hospitals are trying to serve a growing population from a shrinking subsidy base—essentially caring for more with less. It is only a matter of time before public hospitals fail to meet their traditional charter of caring for the poor because we—*as a society*—are not doing enough.

We have two choices. As a society, we can provide the tax dollars necessary to bail out the public hospitals in hopes they can continue to meet their mission to the poor. Or, we can come up with an alternative solution that spreads the cost across a larger tax base and the delivery across a larger provider base. Ideally we could do both . . .

The health care industry has a brief window of opportunity to put its house in order . . . to make the competitive marketplace workable . . . and to come to terms with critical issues such as uncompensated care. However, if the health care poor can't get care from their local doctors and hospitals, and if patient "dumping" becomes a widespread practice, the American public may become disenchanted with the new competitive environment in health care. The potential always exists that Congress and state legislatures could react by effectively nationalizing the industry.

Therefore, now is *not* the time to bombard Washington, D.C. with the concerns of special interest groups. Congress is attempting to unite as never before around the single purpose of slashing costs. While the health care industry has done and will do its fair share to reduce our nation's deficit, we also must do our fair share to raise our nation's level of awareness about uncompensated care. We must unite, as an industry, around the fact that severe and arbitrary budget reductions could adversely impact the quality and access to health care—for the health care poor and for all Americans.

Adequate Health Care

Again, equal health care for all is not a realistic goal; but adequate health care for all is possible with coherent health care policy. We must get this message across to the American people and we must hold government ultimately responsible.

In closing, let me suggest that we find ourselves at the proverbial crossroads. For all our passed efforts, an entire segment of the population we have attempted to reach still manages to fall through the cracks. And in today's more competitive environment, those cracks are growing wider and deeper.

Our country desperately needs the proper mix of free market incentives and enlightened government participation to address the problem. Up to now, attempts to legislate health care have been one-sided: First, legislating the entitlement programs that created the massive demand for health care—with little regard to cost; now legislating the budgetary reductions that attempt to curb the runaway cost of entitlements—with little regard to the negative impact on quality and access.

It's high time to see if government—with counsel and guidance from the health care industry—can legislate a program that strikes a better balance between social and economic needs. *That's* the challenge we face. And whether it's the 99th Congress or state and local government that finally bites the bullet and leads the way, nearly 30 million Americans are in the hospital waiting room hoping we can meet that challenge, a challenge that will endure as long as a single pregnant mother in need of medical attention is stranded on the outside of this vast health care system looking in.

17 PRIVATIZING HEALTH CARE FOR THE POOR

MEDICARE SHOULD BE PRIVATIZED

Peter J. Ferrara, JD

Peter J. Ferrara is an attorney in private practice in Washington, DC, and is well-known as a conservative spokesman on health care issues.

Points to Consider

1. What are the near-term dangers to the Medicare program?
2. How has the system of reimbursement used by Medicare contributed to waste and inefficiency?
3. How has the Prospective Payment System (PPS) affected the quality of care?
4. How would the proposed Slaughter plan function?
5. How would the need for catastrophic coverage be met?
6. What would be the effect on total federal expenditures of the private account system?

Peter J. Ferrara, "To Save Medicare We Must Privatize", *Conservative Digest,* February, 1987. Reprinted by permission of the Conservative Digest.

*With the government paying the medical bills
through Medicare, both doctors and patients tend
to lose concern for costs.*

The Medicare program is going to pieces. The latest annual report of the Social Security Board of Trustees indicates that the program will run short of funds to pay promised benefits sometime in the 1990s, possibly as early as 1993. By the time those now entering the work force retire, under the report's most widely cited intermediate projections, Medicare payroll taxes would only be sufficient to pay about forty percent of the promised hospital-insurance benefits. Paying all promised benefits under these projections would require increasing the payroll-tax rate for Medicare by 250 percent.

Under the so-called pessimistic (but often more realistic) projections, payroll-tax revenues would only be sufficient to pay about 20 percent of promised hospital-insurance benefits for today's young workers. Paying all promised benefits for these workers under the projections would require increasing the Medicare payroll-tax rate more than 500 percent, to a level higher than that for all of Social Security and Medicare today.

Medicare spending already totals about $70 billion a year. By the end of this decade, Medicare will be spending almost $100 billion per year—about eight percent of the Federal Budget and a sum equal to total federal appropriations as late as 1963.

The fact is that the Medicare system is responsible for substantial waste and inefficiency, which contribute to the program's long-term financial problems. With the government paying the medical bills through Medicare, both doctors and patients tend to lose concern for costs. Medical consumers have little incentive to seek out the lowest-cost medical service providers, and this weakens competitive pressures for efficiency and for the development of low-cost medical-service alternatives. Doctors and hospitals no longer need to be as concerned about whether their patients can afford the charges, and consequently may charge more than they otherwise would.

More Regulation

In an attempt to control spiraling costs, and reduce waste and inefficiency, the government has resorted to a sharp increase in

A "Bang-up" Job

Who in his right mind would expect the folks who've done such a bang-up job of delivering our mail, improving our schools, revitalizing our cities, and developing new sources of energy to create any less than a full-fledged disaster area in the field of health care?

Jeff Riggenback, *USA Today,* March 13, 1986

regulation over the private medical community through adoption in 1983 of the Prospective Payment System (P.P.S.) for payment of hospital services. Under this system, the government sets the fees it will pay for treatment of each illness under Medicare, and prohibits doctors and hospitals from charging the patients any more. If the doctor or hospital can provide the treatment for less than the government-set fee, they may keep the difference.

The P.P.S. requirements follow a typical policy pattern pursued by governments deeply involved in financing costly medical treatment for average citizens—sacrificing quality for cost savings. The P.P.S. creates powerful incentives for medical providers to take shortcuts and to shortchange medical consumers in the quality of care. Even if the patient wants to pay more for less-harried service and more personal attention, he can't. Hospitals and doctors can maximize income only by processing all patients as quickly and cheaply as possible. Patients who are slow to respond to treatment may quickly find themselves icily classified as hopeless. Media reports and congressional hearings have already begun to echo complaints of early hospital exits and other forms of harried or inadequate treatment attributable to P.P.S.

Moreover, the Prospective Payment System is slowly evolving into outright price controls, as the government has started to adopt freezes on the P.P.S. fees, and in any event the fees and illness categories each year become more and more outdated and ill-suited to varying local conditions. All of this will naturally tend to reduce the quality and supply of medical care provided under Medicare.

Controls And Costs

Without more fundamental reform, this trend of increasing regulatory controls will only continue, which should be deeply troubling to medical professionals and consumers alike. The result is likely to be more detailed and centralized restrictions on the choices of medical treatment, as well as further attempts to control doctor incomes more directly. As long as Medicare remains primarily a public-sector program, and is therefore highly politicized, the medical profession will be fair game. In the end, both medical-service providers and consumers will be the losers.

The system is also increasingly failing both workers and retirees. Today's workers are being forced to pay ever-increasing taxes into the system, and they lose the benefit of full-market investment returns on those payments, since the funds are not saved and invested in the Medicare trust funds for their future benefits, but are immediately paid out to current beneficiaries.

For the elderly, Medicare co-payment fees increase the longer one stays in the hospital, and these fees are being sharply increased each year. After a certain number of days of hospital care, Medicare coverage stops altogether. By covering routine but not "catastrophic" illnesses, the benefit structure is the inverse of what it should be to serve the true needs and concerns of the elderly.

The Way Out

Fortunately, there is a tremendous opportunity to solve these problems without imposing benefit cuts on the elderly or payroll-tax increases on the young. The solution is sharply to increase the role of the *private sector* in performing the functions of Medicare. Legislation which would do this was introduced last year in the House (H.R. 3505), spearheaded by Representative French Slaughter (R.-Virginia), with over forty co-sponsors, including liberals and conservatives, Democrats and Republicans. Similar legislation may be introduced by several Senate co-sponsors this year. Moreover, President Reagan asked his Administration to study health-care policy options over this year, and his study groups focused on this legislation as one of the main policy alternatives.

Under the proposed legislation, workers would be given the option of substituting private savings and insurance accounts,

By David Seavey, USA TODAY

Copyright *USA Today*. Reprinted with permission.

originally called Health I.R.A.s, for their Medicare coverage, to the extent they individually choose. The House bill called the private alternative "Health Care Savings Accounts," and the Senate bill may call them "Health Pension Accounts." These accounts actually combine the features of I.R.A.s, employer pensions and 402(K) plans.

The legislation specifically provides that workers could contribute to their accounts each year amounts up to the total of the Medicare payroll taxes paid by them and their employers.

Workers would then receive an income-tax credit equal to sixty percent of the amount of such contributions. Employers could make some or all of these contributions for their employees, and receive the 60 percent credit to the extent they did so.

Contributions and investment returns to the account would accumulate tax-free until retirement. After retirement, funds in the account could be used to purchase medical insurance or finance medical expenses directly.

Catastrophe

But there would be government insurance in case of real catastrophe. To the extent each worker and his employers contributed to the private-health account over his working years, an added annual "deductible" would be applied before any payment of Medicare benefits for the worker in retirement. That "deductible" is the amount of medical expenses the retiree is required to meet himself before Medicare pays. For example, if a worker had an added deductible of $1,000 per year, he would be responsible for paying the first $1,000 in medical expenses each year out of his private health account or insurance purchased through that account before the usual Medicare-benefit provisions would apply.

The added deductible would be calculated under a formula determining roughly the amount of health-insurance coverage the worker could be expected to be able to buy each year with funds accumulated in his account, given his record of past contributions and assuming a modest return on investments. The deductible would be higher the more workers or their employers contributed to the private accounts over their careers. A worker contributing the maximum to the account each year of his entire career would have an added annual deductible of $10,000 a year or more.

Since the deductible formula is generous to the worker, he is likely to have more than enough through his private account to finance the added deductible expenses, coming out way ahead on net. Through this added deductible, workers exercising the private-account option would be substituting private savings and insurance for Medicare coverage to the extent they choose.

Workers in retirement could pay themselves cash rebates out of their accounts if they spent less than a specified proportion of the funds on medical expenses or insurance each year or earned

144

more than the modest return on investment assumed in the deductible formula. Workers who exercised the private-account option to at least a certain minimum degree over their careers would receive coverage under Medicare against catastrophic expenses above their annual deductibles. Funds in the private accounts could also be used to finance long-term care in nursing homes or other institutions. Upon death of the worker, either before or after retirement, any remaining funds in the private account would go to the worker's designated heirs . . .

Market Advantage

Further cost savings would result from the increased market competition, improved incentives, and enhanced consumer choices. The new private option would allow private insurers and medical-care providers to compete for coverage of retirees, rather than maintaining the current Medicare monopoly. Private insurers would compete to keep their own costs down by monitoring health providers closely and rooting out wasteful and unnecessary expenditures. Medical-care suppliers would set fees with greater recognition that funds for payment are not inexhaustible. The competition would also increase pressure for development of lower cost medical-care technologies . . .

Complementing this increased competition would be improved incentives for consumers since they will be purchasing services with their own funds in their private accounts. Avoiding unnecessary and overly expensive charges will allow consumers to retain greater reserves in their private accounts and even pay themselves cash rebates. Consumers will consequently devote more effort to seeking out the lowest-cost service providers. They will seek to avoid unnecessary medical care, or care which they themselves feel is not worth the cost. They will devote greater attention to preventive measures which can save medical costs over the long run. The private-account option is a means of bringing natural market incentives back into medicine. Not in a harsh way that may deprive some, but in a positive way that provides enhanced benefits and rewards for responding to market incentives.

Workers would receive full market returns on their private-account investments, unlike through Medicare, and these returns would constitute a new source of funds to meet health-care needs. Workers would also have a new means to address concerns over catastrophic coverage and long-term nursing-home care. Overall, the private account offers workers a highly attractive option through which they could substantially improve their retirement prospects and income . . .

Market Freedoms

For doctors and other medical professionals, the reform offers the advantage of depoliticizing medical care, by moving more of the financing of such care into the private sector. Medical professionals would consequently work under the same market freedoms as other professionals, rather than as targets of government scapegoating campaigns and increased government regulation.

Moreover, the reduced Medicare spending resulting from the private accounts would mean a big reduction in total federal spending, probably greater than President Reagan has been able to achieve through all other efforts combined to date. Yet, this can be accomplished *without* attempting any painful, politically infeasible, benefit cuts, but simply by offering U.S. workers a better deal from within the private sector.

18 PRIVATIZING HEALTH CARE FOR THE POOR

GOVERNMENT COMMITMENT TO MEDICARE SHOULD BE MAINTAINED

Harrison L. Rogers, Jr., M.D.

Dr. Harrison L. Rogers, Jr., is President-Elect of the American Medical Association and a physician in the practice of surgery in Atlanta, Georgia.

Points to Consider

1. What has been the federal involvement in Medicare since its inception?
2. Why is Medicare facing a crisis?
3. What are some major features of this crisis?
4. What are some of the AMA's short-term recommendations for Medicare?
5. How would the Kennedy-Gephardt bill impose rationing?

Excerpted from hearings before the House Subcommittee on Health of the Committee on Ways and Means on the Medicare financing crisis and recommendations for Medicare financial reforms, September 13, 1984.

The creation of the Medicare program in 1965 was a commitment to the elderly that this nation would assure them access to, and meet the major part of the cost of, high quality health care services. To a large extent that promise has been met.

Medicare and Medicaid were enacted at the beginning of a period marked by expansion of federal involvement in social programs. The "Great Society" programs of the mid-sixties embraced new segments of the population and provided a wide array of social services. A variety of health programs were included. For many years "health" was a fundamental issue commanding a prominent place in the political scene. Almost limitless funds were being allocated into varying aspects of the health system:

Basic research was greatly expanded resulting in new scientific breakthroughs in technology.

Hospitals modernized and expanded throughout the country as a result of the Hill-Burton program of federal financial assistance.

Health manpower development burgeoned with expansion of federal assistance to medical and allied health schools and their students.

It is within the context of expanded federal assistance for facility development, for manpower expansion, for health research and dissemination of medical knowledge, and expansion of alternative delivery systems that the federal medical programs providing payment for medical services completed a circle of large-scale encouragement and direct financial support for the health care system.

Development of Medicare

During the decade or so following enactment of Medicare the expectations of the nation's elderly for health care coverage through Medicare grew. These expectations were recognized by the Congress, which reacted to a variety of pressures, including those of an increasing elderly population. Congress expanded the Medicare program, and extended coverage to new population groups—the disabled and those with end-stage renal disease (ESRD). The Congress had clearly made a major commitment to

Medicaid Coverage

The variability among states in Medicaid coverage is clearly associated with substantial differences in access to physicians' services for the poor. The differences are most dramatic for low-income children. Since 40 percent of the nation's poor today are chidren, this finding needs careful attention.

These results support earlier studies showing the value of Medicaid in getting poor people into the medical care system. Public insurance coverage seems to do so considerably more effectively than subsidized or uncompensated care provided by hospitals and clinics.

Robert J. Blendon, *The New England Journal of Medicine,* May 1, 1986

large segments of the U.S. population that high quality care would be made available and paid for. Health care as a "right" became a central theme in the 1970s in discussions on health care. What was created was a situation of expanding beneficiary rolls and increased beneficiary expectations. During this era primary attention was focused on quality rather than costs.

In the main these developments occurred in an era of relative national affluence. But because of program expansion, the cost-based reimbursement methodology, the increase in numbers of Medicare beneficiaries, the rapidly expanding availability of providers, and the growing rate of inflation in the economy as a whole, the costs of Medicare were escalating sharply.

Unfortunately, the economic vitality of the country did not keep pace with increasing demands of federal programs and expenditures. The federal government is now faced with serious economic problems, including growing budget deficits. In the light of many economic, social and technological changes, Medicare is coming under close scrutiny. Because of increasing annual federal deficits, fundamental changes—even the mention of which would have been unthinkable only a few years ago—are now freely discussed in many quarters and are the subject of this hearing today.

Forces Driving Program to Financial Crisis

There are certain basic forces driving the current program toward financial crisis, including: an aging population; high per capita health care costs for the elderly; the decreasing proportion of workers to beneficiaries; the inability of government to financially meet all its obligations and promises; rising total health care costs; expanded medical technology; increasing professional liability costs; and general inflationary measures.

Several important observations in this area are:

In the next fifty years the population over 65 will more than double and the population over 85 will more than triple.

The ratio of workers to elderly will decrease from 5:1 in 1990 to 3:1 in 2025.

As the proportion of older people in the population increases, the requirements for acute and long-term care will increase.

Although the elderly comprise 11% of the total population, they make 30% of all patient visits to office-based physicians.

Forty percent of total hospital inpatient days are used by elderly patients. In 1978 short-stay hospital admissions for persons age 65 and over were about 350 per thousand population, while for those under 65 the figures were about 132 per thousand population. Older patients have an average length of stay 76% greater than younger adults.

The elderly occupy 90% of nursing home beds.

Persons over 65 incurred 3.5 times the per capita health care expenditures of persons under age 65. Almost two-thirds of these expenditures are covered through Medicare and Medicaid.

Over 97% of private nursing home expenditures are out-of-pocket expenses for the aged and their families, uncovered by Medicare or private insurance.

Between 60% and 80% of the long-term care the disabled elderly receive in the community is provided informally by a spouse, other relatives, and/or friends. The presence of a spouse and/or children is the most important factor determining whether or not a disabled elderly patient will enter a nursing home.

Medicare Recommendations

The creation of the Medicare program in 1965 was a commitment to the elderly that this nation would assure them access to, and meet the major part of, the cost of high quality health care services. To a large extent that promise has been met.

The 18 years since the enactment of Medicare have seen tremendous improvement in not only access to and the availability of high quality health care but also in the health care status of the covered population. One of the principal reasons why the Medicare program has been able to accomplish these important twin goals of easy access to high quality care and improved overall health status has been the ability of the Medicare beneficiary to receive care in the same mainstream fashion as other individuals.

The American Medical Association is committed to the provision of the highest possible quality of care for Medicare beneficiaries. To assure the viability of this commitment into the future, the AMA is in the process of conducting a detailed review of the Medicare program to develop recommendations for long-term program modifications. As part of this project, we have developed a series of recommendations designed to help to assure the short-term solvency of the Medicare program. The recommendations include:

A moderate one-time increase in the payroll tax rate on employers and employees.

An increase in the present rates for alcohol and tobacco products with the additional revenues from these new taxes directed to the Hospital Insurance Trust Fund.

Imposing the health insurance tax on the non-wage income of individuals above a certain threshold and up to the taxable maximum.

Imposing a Part A premium on Medicare beneficiaries based on beneficiary income that is above a certain level.

Imposing a coinsurance requirement on beneficiaries for Part A hospital expenses up to a specified cost-sharing limit, with the cost-sharing amount varying according to beneficiary income.

Periodically increasing the age of eligibility for Medicare to reflect changes in longevity, health, and employment status, with special consideration given to the coordination of eligibility dates for Medicare and Social Security cash benefits and a continuation of private health insurance coverage for those who retire prior to attaining Medicare eligibility due to age.

Increasing the Part B premium to a level adequate to fund 35% of costs, with consideration to be given to relating the premium

151

amount to the income status of beneficiaries.

The AMA believes that implementation of those recommendations will provide meaningful program modifications to address the short-term financial problems facing the Medicare program.

The Association is now continuing its intensive review of the Medicare program, as well as overall issues surrounding the delivery of health care for the elderly and disabled for the long-term . . .

Conclusion

The AMA urges this Subcommittee and Congress to continue to recognize the commitment made to the elderly and disabled of this nation—to assure access to high quality medical care. We urge you to carefully evaluate and accept the recommendations we have made for short-term modifications in the Medicare program. We believe that enactment of such modifications can provide sufficient time, free from the pressures of short-term budget and fiscal constraints, to develop appropriate long-term approaches. We are continuing our efforts to identify reforms to assure a comprehensive approach for dealing with the long-term issues concerning the assurance of access to high quality health care for the elderly and disabled.

WHAT IS POLITICAL BIAS?

This activity may be used as an individualized study guide for students in libraries and resource centers or as a discussion catalyst in small group and classroom discussions.

Many readers are unaware that written material usually expresses an opinion or bias. The skill to read with insight and understanding requires the ability to detect different kinds of bias. Political bias, race bias, sex bias, ethnocentric bias and religious bias are five basic kinds of opinions expressed in editorials and literature that attempt to persuade. This activity will focus on political bias defined in the glossary below.

5 KINDS OF EDITORIAL OPINION OR BIAS

sex bias— the expression of dislike for and/or feeling of superiority over a person because of gender or sexual preference

race bias— the expression of dislike for and/or feeling of superiority over a racial group

ethnocentric bias—the expression of a belief that one's own group, race, religion, culture or nation is superior. Ethnocentric persons judge others by their own standards and values.

political bias—the expression of opinions and attitudes about government-related issues on the local, state, national or international level

religious bias—the expression of a religious belief or attitude

Guidelines

Read through the following statements and decide which ones represent political opinion or bias. Evaluate each statement by using the method indicated below.

Mark (P) for statements that reflect any political opinion or bias.

Mark (F) for any factual statements.

Mark (O) for statements of opinion that reflect other kinds of opinion or bias.

Mark (N) for any statements that you are not sure about.

Evaluate statements for biases (P,F,O,N)

___ 1. The dumping of indigent patients by for-profit hospitals is a rare occurrence.

___ 2. When it does happen, it is justified by the 'bottom-line' ethics of the hospital concerned.

___ 3. The investor-owned hospital is just as accountable to the community as the traditional, voluntary hospital.

___ 4. Both for-profit and non-profit hospitals are finding it increasingly difficult to provide for indigent patients.

___ 5. The government's Medicaid program has kept pace with inflation to provide adequate health care coverage for the poor.

___ 6. Before referring indigent emergency patients to public, general hospitals, the law requires that their medical condition first be stabilized.

___ 7. The experience of the poor in using the health care system is largely a result of their own attitudes to the importance of health care.

___ 8. Funding for a national catastrophic health insurance program for the poor and elderly should be a matter for the private insurance industry.

___ 9. Most lower and middle income elderly Americans can obtain full-time nursing home care without having to go into poverty.

___ 10. The Bowen catastrophic health care proposal is consistent with the philosophy of the Reagan Administration.

___ 11. There is no conflict of interest in the arrangements between for-profit hospitals and insurance companies.

___ 12. Many for-profit hospitals are refusing to treat the poor.

___ 13. For-profit hospitals should not be required to give treatment to the poor and indigent.
___ 14. For-profit hospitals will make medical care more efficient.
___ 15. For-profit hospitals will make medical care more expensive and less sensitive to the needs of the poor.
___ 16. Non-profit hospitals are forced to care for a disproportionate share of the poor.
___ 17. Even the most compassionate hospitals are now being forced to choose between rationing health care for the poor or bankruptcy for their institutions.
___ 18. All medical care should be provided without charge through a national medical program.
___ 19. Socialized medicine has never provided quality medical care for the general population.
___ 20. Every person has a right to medical care, even if they cannot afford to pay for it.
___ 21. Today there are 40 million people who are without health insurance.
___ 22. We must have a proper balance between government and private-profit seeking roles in the medical industry.
___ 23. The Reagan administration has not provided adequate funding for medical programs that treat the poor and indigent.

CHAPTER 5

HEALTH CARE SYSTEMS: A GLOBAL PERSPECTIVE

19 HEALTH CARE SYSTEMS: A GLOBAL PERSPECTIVE

OVERVIEW:

THE COMMUNIST SYSTEM
THE SOCIAL DEMOCRATIC SYSTEM
THE CAPITALIST SYSTEM

John L. McFarland

John L. McFarland is a free-lance writer in the Minneapolis, Minnesota area.

Health Care in Socialist (Communist) Countries

In communist countries the overwhelming share of productive capital (factories, tools, buildings, etc.) has been taken over by the state and administered on behalf of the whole people. Production is planned centrally with the requirements of the entire country for capital and consumer goods uppermost. Other countries, which have not proceeded on the Leninist, or Soviet, model but which also call themselves socialist, have only a minimal amount of central planning, so that individual enterprises function like cooperatives internally as far as democratic relations between labor and management are concerned, but relate to each other externally as capitalist businesses would, producing the competitive "market socialism" of Yugoslavia, for example. Most countries that are socialist in the Marxist-Leninist, or Soviet, sense, in addition to domination of the economy by the state sector, still allow a small percentage of private enterprise as long as the number of employees does not exceed a certain limit (12 in the German Democratic Republic (GDR); 35 in Hungary). The profits of such enterprises, however, are closely monitored by the state and taxed to prevent the excessive accumulation of capital that would permit its owners to bid for political power and influence.

Medical services in such a socialist economy are provided as part of what is called the "social wage," which is that fraction of the value of all goods and services allocated to providing social services and subsidizing the prices of necessities. Whenever the net wages directly paid to workers in a socialist country are compared with those of their Western counterparts, more than the mere money value should be borne in mind. The value of the social wage, exemplified by food, housing, transportation, and education, which are heavily subsidized, and health care, which is almost totally subsidized, should be added as well. Rather than imposing payroll or income taxes on citizens to pay for welfare services, the socialist state is in a position to take what it needs directly from production before it reaches the distribution system. In fact, the very concept of welfare for those in danger of falling through some kind of social "safety net" because of unemployment or disability is foreign to socialist societies, since everyone capable of work must contribute to production as an intellectual, agricultural, administrative, or industrial worker. There may be pockets of underemployment or groups of workers whose skills have become superseded by the increasing productivity of industrial robots, for example, but those affected are retrained for new jobs requiring higher skill levels and placed in new jobs. Advanced socialist countries, such as the USSR, the GDR, and Hungary, still reward workers unequal compensation based on their unequal productivity and skills, but the comparatively small income differentials that exist are generally used for discretionary, i.e., non-essential, semi-luxury goods and services. The claim is made, however, that a service as basic as health care is available to all as a right of citizenship, regardless of age, sex, income, ethnic background or social status. Higher-income groups can avail themselves of private care by specialists who "moonlight" outside the state health sector, but the basic no-frills floor of health care available to the general population is conceded by Western observers to be quite adequate for all contingencies.

Health Care in Social Democratic Countries

The break-neck pace of industrialization in late nineteenth-century Germany led to the acceleration of social tensions between the "haves" and "have-nots" that threatened massive unrest if social reforms were not adopted. In order to diffuse the rising militancy of the German working class, many of the features of the welfare state as it exists in Western Europe today were introduced under Bismarck in the 1870s and 1880s. The basic social security law was passed under Kaiser Wilhelm I in 1883. This set in motion a process of accommodation between the monarchy, the aristocracy, the entrepreneurial and working classes on the basis of a multi-party parliamentary system which came to be known as social democracy. The Social Democratic Party (SPD) of West Germany has continually and successfully pressed for and achieved welfare, economic, and social reforms exceeding anything enacted in the United Kingdom (UK) and certainly in the USA.

While the leadership of the social democratic parties has never swerved from support of the free enterprise system, they have overseen such measures to democratize it as in West Germany, for example, a system of labor/management cooperation under which Works Councils are elected by workers in all private businesses that have at least five employees. The Councils represent employees in social, personnel and economic matters. Thus they exercise co-determination with shareholders' representatives in matters of shop organization, working time, the wage pattern, regulations on work safety, occupational illnesses and health protection. The Councils have to be called upon in questions of personnel planning and career training. Under the Chancellorship of Willy Brandt, West Germany also embarked on a policy of detente with socialist countries, especially Poland and the USSR. While the SPD has been out of power, its reforms have remained in place under Christian Democratic governments. The history of post-war Austria and the Scandanavian countries has paralleled that of West Germany to a large extent, especially in terms of welfare and social security legislation, so that they may be classified under the term social democratic.

Health Care in the Capitalist System

Because the provision of medical care varies so much within the capitalist world, this part of the Overview will be restricted to a description of how the American concept of "free enterprise" has shaped our health care system. For example, even the UK, one of our closest ideological allies, has moved both health insurance and the actual delivery of health care itself off the market and into what it calls the National Health Service, a state-funded and administered system whose budget is closely tied to a percentage of the UK's Gross National Product (5.2% in 1975). There is a similarly wide diversity of professional relationships, institutional arrangements, and insurance schemes among all Western (capitalist) health care systems. Our medical system evolved until the 1980s almost exclusively under the control of the physician as private entrepreneur in a fee-for-service relationship with individual patients and, since the 1930s, their private or governmental insurers, and has relied on the community at large to provide the capital outlays required for building and equipping (public or voluntary) hospitals both for in-patient care and the practical training of future physicians.

Our commitment to free enterprise has meant excluding the government from all sectors of the health care industry where profit could be extracted and restricting its involvement to the provision of facilities for physicians mentioned above, mass immunization of schoolchildren, the funding of medical research,

160

By Bill Sanders, *The Milwaukee Journal*, © New America Syndicate, 1985, by permission of North America Syndicate, Inc.

and other aspects of public health having mainly a diagnostic and not a therapeutic nature. Whenever the public health sector has threatened to exceed these bounds and actually provide clinical care, as it did in the early 1900s and then with the Community Health Centers of the 1960s, organized private medicine brought political pressure to bear to reconfine public health to a caretaker role. The physician's concept of free enterprise has traditionally meant resisting the intrusion of any third party into the doctor-patient relationship, be they insurers, bureaucracies, or private corporations seeking to run hospitals with physician-employees for the profit of investors. The philosophy of this approach has been that only the doctor and the patient can freely enter into the medical service transaction, the doctor being the best judge of whether and how the care-seeker should be cared for and at what cost, the patient being the best judge of the value of care received, expressing this judgment by deciding whether or not to establish an on-going relationship with the physician. After considerable resistance from organized medicine, third-party insurance became the norm in the 1930s and 1940s with the "Blues" (Blue Cross for hospital coverage and Blue Shield for doctors' fees). Although these plans helped prevent over-use by patients with built-in deductibles and co-insurance, they did not reflect any concern for cost-effectiveness, which had characterized the traditional two-party arrangement, and provided a green light for the inflation of doctor and hospital fees.

The entry by shareholder-owned for-profit corporations into the practice of medicine did not become significant in this country until the 1980s, after a prolonged period of seemingly uncontrollable inflation in the 1970s associated with traditional cost-plus reimbursement. In an effort to rein in burgeoning costs, payors began to mandate maximum levels of patient benefits and an end to the practice by hospitals of subsidizing care for the indigent by padding everyone else's bill. Hospitals built with Hill-Burton funding were legally obligated to treat indigent patients, and these typically have been the larger, general, public hospitals near city centers. This has provided a two-pronged disincentive for newer, especially investor-owned, hospitals, to handle indigent cases at all, although many claim to furnish this service to the community. After the indigent patient's (generally emergency) condition has stabilized, the contention is that many for-profit hospitals then ship them to a general hospital. The alleged rich/poor or two-tier health care disparity has thus been widened in the 1980s.

Health care for the poor now falls with increasing severity on already overtaxed governmental funding programs, such as Medicaid. Adopted in 1965 along with Medicare, the two programs reflect sharply different philosophies. As a system of health insurance for the elderly, Medicare fit in with the well-established tradition of Social Security and enjoys uniform national standards for eligibility and benefits. Medicare, although originally opposed by physicians, allowed them to charge above what the program would pay and thus lent itself to abuse and fed inflation. Medicaid was associated with the stigma of charity, reimbursement was strictly limited and participation among physicians was far more limited, and it was left to the states to decide how adequate their programs would be. The failure of Medicare to cover long-term nursing home care for the elderly forces them to "spend down" into poverty by unloading their assets in order to qualify for Medicaid, which in 1982 paid over 50% of all nursing home expenditures nationally. Thus the Medicaid program is even less able to care for the non-elderly indigent because of this gap in Medicare, covering only 40% of those falling under the federal definition of poor by the mid-1980s.

Even with the severe cost containment measures that have been adopted by policy makers at the Federal level and which have been forced on the states by the "New Federalism" of the Reagan Administration, the inflation of physician and hospital fees has continued to outstrip the annual increase in the Consumer Price Index significantly. Even conservative commentators have conceded the likelihood of the U.S. being forced to adopt a system of state control as well as state funding, with the rationing of care based not on the wealth of the care-seeker but on bureaucratic priorities.

20 HEALTH CARE SYSTEMS: A GLOBAL PERSPECTIVE

HEALTH CARE IN A COMMUNIST SOCIETY

The German Democratic Republic
Ministry of Health

The following statement was taken from a publication of the German Democratic Republic (GDR) Ministry of Health describing the health care industry in East Germany.

Points to Consider

1. What health measures were undertaken in the Soviet zone of occupation (in what later became East Germany) in the 1940s?
2. What has been the GDR's strategy for health care in the 1980s?
3. What are the responsibilities of the Ministry of Health?
4. Are people free to choose their own personal physician?
5. What services are provided by the natal clinics?
6. How are the elderly helped to remain independent?

Excerpted from *Health Care in the German Democratic Republic,* published by the GDR Ministry of Health, 1984.

Into the 1960s the major tasks were to place increased emphasis on preventive measures, and to improve public health standards in workplaces and residential areas.

In the aftermath of the Second World War, a complicated situation had arisen on the territory of what is now the GDR. Working and living conditions were almost disastrous. Famine and epidemics were stalking the streets . . .

Major changes were initiated in the health system. They were largely based on the health policy guidelines adopted in March 1947 by the Socialist Unity Party of Germany (which had emerged from the merger of Communists and Social Democrats in 1946). Within a few years of the German people's liberation from facism, the worst consequences of the war had been overcome. The general state of health improved, epidemics were brought under control, and major advances were made in establishing a public health service accessible to all. To create the necessary material safeguards for the working class and all other members of the working population, a uniform social insurance system was introduced and insurance made compulsory for all wage-earners and salaried employees. Hospitals were rebuilt and, in a parallel development, the first health centers and outpatient departments set up.

With the aid of Soviet doctors the authorities began to establish an industrial health service in 1947, the first time such a task was undertaken in Germany. From the outset, they gave special attention to maternal and child care. Centrally administered organizations with specialist clinics were brought into existence to combat tuberculosis and venereal diseases . . .

During the 1950s the main object was to lay the foundations for a socialist health service on a large scale and to expand them systematically. Into the 1960s the major tasks were to raise health care standards as a responsibility of the whole community, to place increased emphasis on preventive measures, and to improve public health standards in workplaces and residential areas. Under the reform of higher education initiated in 1951, academic research and teaching were geared to the requirements of scholarship imbued with a humanistic spirit and reflecting the interests of the working people.

One reason the GDR health service developed without

encountering major obstacles was that the support of the medical community was enlisted each time a new challenge had to be met. The 1950s saw the laying of the foundations of socialism and furnished clear evidence that this social system offered vast opportunities for the medical profession . . .

The Constitution of the GDR stipulates in Article 35:

1. All citizens of the German Democratic Republic shall be entitled to the protection of their health and working capacity.
2. This right shall be guaranteed by the systematic improvement of working and living conditions, public health measures, a comprehensive social policy, and the promotion of physical culture, school and mass sport, and outdoor recreation.
3. Material security, medical aid and medicines, and other medical services shall be provided free of charge in the event of illness or accident on the basis of a social insurance system . . .

Health Care Priorities

The most recent health policy decisions focus attention on tasks designed to achieve noticeable improvements in medical services for the vast majority of the population and thus to raise the general state of health. Priority is being given to strengthening the system of primary health care.

Health and social services figure prominently among the far-reaching objectives and tasks derived from the economic strategy for the 1980s and the social policy program based on it. The following aspects deserve special mention:

● The quality and efficiency of medical and social services ensure that all citizens enjoy a sense of security and well-being in their country. They are aware that everything humanly possible is being done to help them.

● The standard of the health and social services provided has an indirect influence on the raising of economic performance levels.

● All health and social workers use the possibilities at their command to encourage healthy living . . .

Organization

The Ministry of Health is the government department charged with the administration and planning of health and social services.

Millions of Unnecessary Deaths

Millions of unnecessary deaths worldwide could be prevented through simple and relatively inexpensive health care measures, a study by a Washington research group said Saturday.

"Though their health care needs differ drastically, the rich and the poor do have one thing in common: both die unnecessarily," said William Chandler in the study "Improving World Health: A Least Cost Strategy."

Associated Press, July, 1984

The principal functions of the Minister of Health are to:

● supervise the execution of health policy with special regard for the systematic and balanced development of medical services and to make sure all social services assigned to the Ministry as well as medical research and public health measures are carried out as planned;

● make provision for medical care geared to the growing needs of the population and reflecting the latest advances in medicine, with equal emphasis being laid on prevention, diagnosis, therapy and follow-up care;

● ensure that the demand for drugs, medical equipment and other products essential to medical and social services is satisfied;

● further socialist economic integration among the member countries of the Council for Mutual Economic Assistance and develop international cooperation in the field of health . . .

Most institutions in the GDR that provide health and social services are run by the state, with all those working there having the status of employees. But denominational and private facilities also have a part to play within the context of the health system . . .

Medical and Social Services

The emphasis is on primary care, both hospital-based and outpatient. Primary care comprises all medical services—prevention, diagnosis, treatment and rehabilitation—that are by now available, as a rule, to the residents of every district and that are used most frequently by them. Because of its extraordinary significance for a majority of the population it figures high on the list of priorities, all the more so as it largely determines the general standard of medical care.

All patients are free to consult a doctor, often a family practitioner, of their own choice. There has emerged a new doctor-patient relationship free of commercial interests. General practitioners play a key role in the development of primary care and of the family doctor system. They handle nearly half of all new cases and consultations and carry out over 90 per cent of all visits to patients' homes arranged by state-run outpatients units. It should be mentioned that general practitioners are specialists in their own right with qualifications matching those of doctors engaged in other specialist fields . . .

Prevention is a cardinal principle of the medical profession. It is at the center of the system of health surveillance, which covers patients suffering or at risk from certain cardiovascular diseases, kidney ailments, rheumatism, diabetes, cancer and tuberculosis as well as various occupational diseases. Preventive health care focuses on:

● improving health care for pregnant women, mothers and children;

● improving health care for the working population;

● extending measures to prevent infections;

● moving gradually towards the early detection and treatment or, preferably, prevention of certain types of disease (e.g. cardiovascular diseases, malignant tumors and neurological disorders);

● and adopting more effective measures to encourage healthy living.

The many programs that have been initiated to combat selected diseases form an essential component of preventive health care. The programs to control hypertension, myocardiac infarction, cancer and diabetes deserve special mention here . . .

Outpatient Services

Health centers (Polikliniken) form the backbone of outpatient care. Administered by the state, they have at least the following units:

● a general department plus medical, surgical, gynecological, pediatric and dental units;

168

- an X-ray diagnosis unit;
- a laboratory for diagnostic purposes;
- a physiotherapy unit.

Outpatient clinics (Ambulatorien), which are also run by the state, have at least three specialist units.

The network of outpatient facilities providing primary health care is supplemented by state-run medical practices and by doctors in private practice. District nurses, who are employed by the state, play a pivotal role by administering first aid to accident victims and other patients and dispensing treatment prescribed by a doctor. While working under the supervision of a medical practitioner, they depend much on their own initiative, their responsibilities including both preventive care and social services. District nurses visit patients in their homes, proffer advice and care for the sick . . .

Hospital Services

Hospitals occupy an important place in the integrated system of outpatient and inpatient services. Administered by the state, they are increasingly developing into diagnostic and therapeutic centers of the local area in which they are situated. As a rule, hospitals have health centers attached to them . . .

Their principal function is to provide services for inpatients, which includes preventive, diagnostic, therapeutic and rehabilitative measures as well as obstetric services. One of their tasks is to influence the quality and efficiency of medical care in the local area through systematic guidance and information and through postgraduate training . . .

Primary medical care is supplemented by specialist and highly specialized care. Specialist care comprises those medical services which, as a rule, are not available in every district but in every county, e.g. the implantation of artificial joints and pacemakers and artificial kidney treatment (dialysis). In 1983, dialysis was performed almost 170,000 times, and 252 out of every million inhabitants had a pacemaker inserted for the first time.

Maternal and Child Care

Maternal and child services are provided by 900-odd antenatal clinics where expectant mothers are examined periodically. More than 99 per cent of all deliveries take place in obstetrical hospital wards. While they are still in the maternity hospital, all newborn babies are examined for phenylketonuria and vaccinated against tuberculosis.

After their discharge from the obstetrical ward all children are regularly examined in post-natal clinics. There are 10,000 such clinics which hold nearly three million consultations each year, most of them with a doctor in charge. Everything humanly possible is done to monitor and further the development of infants and young children through systematic preventive measures and the provision of social services. Special attention is given to instructing mothers in the art of caring for and feeding a baby. Within a week of being discharged from hospital, mothers are visited in their homes by child welfare officers. Such home visits, which are especially important after the birth of a first child, are meant to give parents informed advice.

Facilities for children between five months and three years of age, known as creches, are part of the system of health and social services. Creches cater for the children of parents who are in employment or attending college. Their main purpose is to look after their health, which includes regular medical attention, and to develop their mental and physical capacities . . .

Care of the Elderly

The GDR has a relatively high proportion of elderly people, whose welfare is an important concern of their family and of socialist society as a whole. The significant contribution which these people have made to the development of our country has earned them the respect and solicitude they deserve. This enables them to play an active part in the life of the community, in a climate of material and emotional security, up to a ripe old age. Society, and specifically the authorities, the trade unions and other mass organizations are doing their utmost to help the elderly lead a rich and rewarding life . . .

Old people's and nursing homes provide residential accommodation for those people who on account of their age or state of health need specialized care and attention. They look after their well-being, arrange for medical care and organize social and cultural activities. The charge is a modest 105 marks at most for old people's homes and up to 120 marks a month for nursing homes. Most of the costs incurred are borne by the state. At the end of 1983 there were about 1,400 old people's and nursing homes with a total capacity of 132,000, i.e. over 30,000 more than in 1970. In line with demand, the number of places involving nursing care has been raised in particular, the current proportion being 65 per cent of the total.

Whereas 29 places per 1,000 people of pensionable age were available in 1971, this figure had risen to 45 by 1983. Extensive repair and modernization schemes have led to major improvements in the conditions provided in older homes.

Close attention is also being given to specially designed housing for old people who do not live in a home. Purpose-built residential blocks provided as part of the housing program enable senior citizens to maintain an independent life for as long as possible. These blocks contain flatlets with all modern conveniences as well as common rooms, laundries and other shared facilities. The modernization of older housing estates begun in recent years has also helped bring about better living conditions for the elderly . . .

Finance

As medical and social services grow in importance, the outlay involved increases in equal measure. Expenditure has, in fact, risen faster than the growth rate of the country's national income in recent years. Spending on medical care, including social insurance spending on drugs, appliances and physiotherapy, took up over five per cent of national income in 1983. About half the funds allocated went into outpatient care.

Under the terms of the GDR Constitution there exists a comprehensive social insurance system run by the trade unions on behalf of factory and office workers, as the labor movement had long demanded should be established.

Social Insurance

Two social insurance programs are in operation:
● The first, open to wage-earners and salaried employees and covering 90 per cent of the population, is administered by the Confederation of Free German Trade Unions.
● The second program, run by the state, is reserved for members of agricultural and craft cooperatives, self-employed people and other groups.

The social insurance budget forms part of the national budget. The funds required come from insurance contributions and payments by firms and the state . . .

The insurance coverage provided for all employees and their dependents means that medical care is accessible to all free of charge. In other words, all citizens have the same right to health care regardless of their social origin, situation or place of residence. The extent and nature of medical aid is determined solely by the patient's condition.

Spending on Selected State-Administered Health & Social Services
(1960 = 100%)

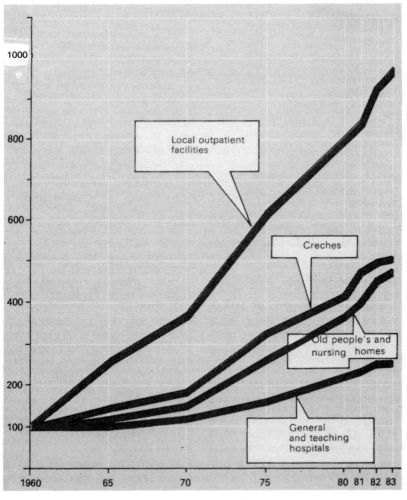

21 HEALTH CARE SYSTEMS: A GLOBAL PERSPECTIVE

HEALTH CARE IN THE WELFARE STATE

The Swedish Institute

The following statement was taken from a publication of the Swedish Institute describing the health care industry in Sweden.

Points to Consider

1. What have been some of the milestones in the evolving Swedish health care system?
2. How much dental and medical care are provided privately in Sweden?
3. When does the state medical system require fees from patients?
4. Where do subsidies for the health care system come from?
5. If cost is a factor in treatment, how is free care provided?

Excerpted from *The Evolution of Social Welfare Policy in Sweden* and "Fact Sheets on Sweden" provided by the Swedish Institute, 1986.

Health care is regarded in Sweden as being clearly a task for the public sector. Like social welfare services, it is provided mainly by local authorities.

Voluntary sickness and unemployment insurance organizations appeared in Sweden in the late 1880s mainly covering gainfully employed men. The characteristic feature of reform work in the field of social insurance between the end of World War II and the 1960s was that the public sector assumed a clear responsibility for people's economic security and expanded social insurance systems to cover all inhabitants of Sweden.

Historical Background

The laws concerning medical care that were enacted at the beginning of the 20th century were virtually all integrated into one uniform piece of legislation in 1928. The county councils were assigned the responsibility for health care which they still have today.

The 1930s witnessed the beginning of a long period of change and development in Swedish health care. The latest change is the new Health and Medical Care Act which went into effect January 1, 1983.

Legislation

Medical care legislation has been amended every decade. In 1940 it was a question of incorporating certain special regulations into the legislation and achieving uniform administration of hospital care. In 1959 uniform legislation was passed which covered both somatic care and that sector of the psychiatric medical care services operated by the county councils and three municipalities outside county council jurisdiction (Gothenburg, Malmö and Gotland). Amendments to the 1959 acts passed in 1962 contained regulations on outpatient care, because the district medical officer system of outpatient care was placed under the jurisdiction of the county councils. The system had previously been run by the State since the 17th century. In 1967 the county councils also took over responsibility for psychiatric care from the State.

The 1968 Act on Protection against Contagious Diseases, which replaced the Epidemic Act of 1919, states that a person who has a transmittable illness such as tuberculosis and venereal disease is legally obliged to submit to medical care and treatment.

In 1980 the position of patients in the health care system was strengthened by the passage of laws on supervision of health care personnel and on complaints committees.

Change and Expansion

The change in the health care system which began in the 1930s also included expansion of public responsibility. During the 1930s, district medical care (care provided by nurses in people's homes plus preventive health care) was granted State subsidies, and the county councils were put in charge. Preventive maternity and child care facilities also began to be expanded. The first legislation on abortions was passed in 1938. A sign of change in people's views on sexuality was that in 1942, sexual education programs were started in the schools, admittedly on a voluntary basis. During the 1940s, laws were also passed concerning sterilization and castration. Current legislation on abortions dates from 1975 and for sterilization from 1976. The school health service started in the 1940s.

Psychiatric care facilities underwent an expansion process during the 1930s. In 1936 the government began to pay subsidies to institutions that took care of the "easily managed mentally ill."

The mid-1940s saw the creation of psychiatric child and youth care centers, mostly in the form of outpatient clinics. During the 1950s there was an additional increase in the number of beds at State hospitals for the mentally ill. At the same time, the nature of psychiatric illnesses was being re-examined, among other things because of the declining influence of the Church, and also because medicines to combat psychiatric illnesses were being developed. A program for care of the mentally ill in families was expanded, and treatment periods were shortened through use of the new drugs. Psychiatric wards were also established at general hospitals, along with psychiatric outpatient clinics. Psychiatric child and youth care was also expanded. As a result of these developments, the county councils took over responsibility for psychiatric care from the State in 1967. At the same time, a new law was passed specifying the conditions under which a person can be committed to involuntary institutional psychiatric care.

Special care for the mentally retarded was long neglected. Aside from limited legislation in 1944, it was only in 1954 that a law was passed regarding education and care of the mentally retarded. The county councils were assigned responsibility. The current act on special care for certain mentally retarded people dates from 1967. This law has brought about not only a major increase in resources, but also dramatic changes in the care provided. Among other things, the mentally retarded were moved out from institutions to communal homes located in towns. As of 1983, the law was being reviewed, among other things to determine whether the municipalities should assume greater responsibility for the mentally retarded.

In 1951 the county councils were assigned responsibility for long-term care of the chronically ill. Long-term care had until 1951 been inadequate and had been provided in homes for the elderly and similar institutions, before that in poorhouses. Long-term care underwent improvements in the 1950s, but especially during the 1960s as a result of 1964 legislation creating special loan support for the expansion of long-term medical care facilities.

Private medical care, mainly on an outpatient basis, exists on a small scale in Sweden.

In principle, medical care in Sweden is free of charge. A person pays a small sum for outpatient care. The national insurance system pays part of medical costs. State appropriations cover other expenses. Most of the costs are paid by the county councils through taxation.

Company health services have been largely unregulated by law. Their aims and structure are regulated by agreements between labor and management organizations. Certain rules are, however, found in the National Insurance Act and in the 1977 Work Environment Act.

The public dental service is operated by each county council and by the three municipalities outside county council jurisdictions. The counties are divided into districts, each of which is supposed to have at least one public dental clinic. Each county is supposed to have a central clinic for more advanced dental work.

As recently as 1971, Sweden's pharmacies were reorganized into one single company, Apoteksbolaget, two-thirds of which is owned by the State and one-third by the pharmacists' association. Before that, pharmacies were entirely private enterprises subject to strict quality control, with personal privileges for pharmacists. Certain price controls were introduced in 1936.

National Health Insurance

Health care is regarded in Sweden as being clearly a task for the public sector. Like social welfare services, it is provided mainly by local authorities . . .

Private health care exists on a limited scale. Only about 5% of physicians work full-time in private practice. The corresponding figure for dentists, however, is more than 50%. Within the inpatient sector there is a limited number of private medical care institutions, chiefly private nursing homes for long-term care . . .

A national health insurance system, financed by the State (to a small extent) and by employer's payroll fees, came into being in 1955. Nowadays it provides medical, sickness, and parental benefits. It covers all Swedish citizens and alien residents.

The health insurance system is mainly an instrument for creating greater socio-economic equality. It enables people with small economic resources and/or extensive medical care needs to take advantage of health care services on the same basis as others. The insurance system moreover functions as a financing instrument and as an instrument of state control.

Medical benefits are payable for physicians' care (on both a public and private outpatient basis), dental treatment, hospital treatment, paramedical treatment such as physiotherapy, convalescent care, handicap aids, and travel expenses. Compensation may also be paid for drugs, non-durable items, and advisory services on birth control, abortion or sterilization.

According to the health insurance rules, the patient pays SEK 55[1] to the county council (including laboratory tests, etc.) for each visit to a doctor at a public outpatient clinic. The doctors themselves receive their entire salaries from the county council. In accordance with a reform of the national health insurance system, which took effect in 1985, the county councils receive compensation from the State in proportion to the number of inhabitants in their respective area. A doctor in private practice is normally entitled to charge the patient about SEK 55 per visit, while in addition receiving a payment from the county council in accordance with separate agreements. In passing the law authorizing the reform, Parliament indicated that the services

---

[1] SEK 1 (Swedish Krona) = .13 U.S. dollar. 55 SEK equals approximately $7.15.

provided by full-time private practitioners will continue as previously. On the other hand, the reform is expected to lead to a substantial reduction in the volume of care provided on a part-time private basis by publicly employed doctors.

A patient pays a maximum of SEK 55 for drugs prescribed by a doctor on any one occasion. The rest is covered by national health insurance. Drugs of life-saving character are provided free of charge.

In 1971, Sweden's pharmacies were reorganized into one single company, *Apoteksbolaget,* two-thirds of which are owned by the State and one-third by the pharmacists' association.

At least 40% of a person's dental costs are covered by the health insurance system.

Sickness benefits provide all Swedish residents with guaranteed protection against loss of income due to illness, injury or handicap. The benefit amounts to 90% of the job income a person normally earns, up to a certain ceiling. Voluntary insurance is available for students and housewives.

Under the *parental insurance system,* parents are, in connection with childbirth, legally entitled to twelve months' leave of absence between them, including nine months with a parental benefit that is equivalent to the sickness benefit and three months with a lower fixed daily allowance. A parent without paid employment receives this fixed daily allowance for the entire twelve-month period.

National Cost

Health care costs have increased very rapidly in recent decades. Today they amount to an estimated SEK 70,000 million, equivalent to about 10% of the gross domestic product, as against about 3% in 1960.

During the past 15 years, these expenses have climbed by 15–20% annually in current prices. During the 1970s, it was possible to keep the cost increase in fixed prices at somewhat more than 4% per year. However, in recent years the increase has been about 2%.

The health care system is financed primarily through county council income taxes, which each county council is entitled to levy on the population of its area. These taxes are proportional, i.e. they represent a given percentage of a person's taxable income, regardless of its size. Between 1960 and 1983, the average county council tax grew from about 4.5% to 13%.

The county council taxes cover about 64% of the costs of the health care system. General state subsidies to level out differences in income among the various county councils add roughly 14%. The remaining sources of income are other state grants, including those for medical education and research and psychiatry (10%), compensation from the national health insurance system (8%), and patients' fees (4%) . . .

Social insurance forms the heaviest element of Swedish social welfare policy, which includes the health and medical services, family benefits and other benefits of various kinds.

Social insurance is defined to include medical, dental and parental insurance, partial, basic and supplementary pensions— all of which come under the National Insurance Act *(Lag om allmän försäkring)*—as well as compulsory work injuries insurance and voluntary unemployment insurance . . .

Allowances for Medical Expenses

This is the collective term covering the various payments which are made in connection with medical attendance, hospital treatment, dental treatment, etc. As a rule these allowances are directly paid by the social insurance office to the health care administration or the individual practitioner responsible for the treatment. Usually, the patient is charged a modest fee at the consultation.

A uniform tariff applies to the public *outpatient services* (as provided by district medical officers and at hospitals). This means that the patient pays SEK 55 for visiting a doctor. Visits to private practitioners come under a separate reimbursement list fixed by the government. As a rule the patient pays SEK 55 out of his own pocket for each visit.

The fees paid by patients cover not only a visit to the doctor, whether he be a public employee or a private practitioner, but also include the following items: issuance of a prescription and a doctor's certificate to qualify for sickness benefit; X-ray and laboratory examinations to which the patient is referred; X-ray, radium and other treatments to which the patient is referred; referral to a specialist with no charge made for a first visit.

180

Allowances for *hospital treatment* in connection with illness or maternity are directly paid by the social insurance office to the county council and usually amount to SEK 55 per day. The patient is not required to pay anything more if treated in a hometown hospital.

A maximum fee of SEK 25 is payable for *paramedical treatment,* i.e. for treatment given by someone other than a physician. The following are regarded as examples of paramedical treatment: physiotherapy, speech therapy (phoniatrics), occupational therapy and psychotherapy. Therapists must be employees of the public medical services. In addition, the treatment is to be prescribed by a licensed medical practitioner.

A similar tariff system is in force for physiotherapy provided by a physiotherapist in private practice. The patient pays a fee of SEK 30 per visit . . .

Rebates are given on *pharmaceutical preparations* (officially registered drugs). The maximum sum payable by the prescription holder at any one time is SEK 55. Pharmacies receive the difference from the social insurance office. No charge is made for drugs in the life-saving category, i.e. pharmaceutical preparation needed to treat chronic and serious diseases.

For persons with considerable costs for medical treatment and pharmaceutical preparations there is a "15-card" which entitles them to free treatment and/or preparations after the 15th visit or purchase and during the twelve months following the date on which the card was issued.

Dental Care

Health insurance also extends to *dental care,* defined to include not only all forms of treatment but also prophylaxis. Its benefits cover the treatment given by members of the public dental service as well as the vast majority of dentists in private practice. The dentists must adhere to an established tariff whose rates may not be exceeded.

At most the patient pays 60% of the costs to the dental service, provided these do not exceed SEK 2,500 in the course of any one treatment period. The dentist is directly reimbursed for the rest from the social insurance office. Where the costs exceed SEK 2,500 for one treatment period, the patient will pay 60% of the cost which amounts to SEK 2,500 and 25% of the cost above this amount.

Children are entitled to free care of their teeth from the public dental service until they reach the age of 16. In some county council jurisdictions the public dental service has been expanded to make free treatment available to those who have reached the ages of 17, 18 and even 19.

HEALTH CARE SYSTEMS: A GLOBAL PERSPECTIVE

HEALTH CARE IN THE FREE MARKET SYSTEM

American Hospital Association

The following article was excerpted from Hospitals, *the official journal of the American Hospital Association.*

Points to Consider

1. What three important events occurred just prior to 1936?
2. What health policies did President Harry Truman, Lyndon Johnson and John F. Kennedy pursue?
3. How has social tension forged our national health policy?
4. How and why have Americans been surprised by the results of national health policies?

"Fifty years of U.S. Health Care Policy," *Hospitals.* Reprinted by permission from *Hospitals,* Vol. 60, No. 9, May 5, 1986. Copyright 1986, American Hospital Association.

When *Hospitals* replaced the old *Bulletin of the American Hospital Association* in January 1936, three events had recently occurred that would influence much of the next 50 years of U.S. health care:

● The Social Security Act passed in 1935, inaugurating a new era of federal involvement in the welfare of at least some U.S. citizens. Although the Social Security Commission recommended that health care for the elderly be part of the package, it was not included.

● The age of private hospitalization insurance began, through the work of C. Rufus Roem, Ph.D., The Committee on the Cost of Medical Care, the American Hospital Association, and the many other pioneering entities that made what would be known as "Blue Cross plans" a reality. Insurance for physicians' services would follow a similar track.

● Largely (but not exclusively) as a result of the work of Sidney Garfield, M.D., in designing health services for migrant construction crews in the West, the idea of health maintenance organizations (or HMOs) was born, soon to be adopted by industrialist Henry J. Kaiser.

These three trends foreshadowed much of what would follow. The period from 1936 to 1945 was marked by growth of Blue Cross and Blue Shield on the one hand and the Kaiser-Permanente model on the other. If Blue Cross and Blue Shield were creatures of the Depression, Kaiser was a creature of World War II and the health care needs of industrial workers.

Government, preoccupied with depression and war, was not very active in health care during this period, although one hallmark event did take place. In 1943, Congress passed the Emergency Maternal and Infant Care Act in order to ensure that health care was available to dependents of low-ranking servicemen. And in the background, there were stirrings of interest in national health insurance (NHI).

The United States began the decade between 1946 and 1955 with a new—and only marginally popular—president, the end of a devastating world war, and the beginning of a period of unparalleled prosperity. It was a golden era for prepaid health insurance. During the war, Congress exempted health-insurance benefits from the wartime freeze on wages; the continued tax

National Health Insurance

Great Britain has had national health insurance for 38 years. Studies of the system have found that its inequalities are far from diminishing and, in some cases, they may be increasing. Other studies have documented widespread inequalities in health care in Sweden and Canada.

John C. Goodman, *USA Today*, March 13, 1986

benefits of employer-provided health insurance helped Blue Cross, Blue Shield, and indemnity plans increase their coverage of the U.S. population. National contracts became a reality as the Blue Cross and Blue Shield plans organized as associations.

A 25-Year Battle for NHI

Yet concurrent with the triumph of private insurance, Harry S. Truman became the first president to endorse NHI. It was the first shot in what would be a 25-year legislative battle. The concept had been around since the 19th century, but Truman's call indicated a new level of support for it. Like all NHI proponents to date, Truman would be frustrated in his efforts.

Other federal health care proposals would be more successful. The Hospital Survey and Construction Act, more popularly known as the Hill-Burton legislation, passed in 1948, providing funds for hospital construction in return for guarantees of care for the poor. In 1950, in an action that drew little notice at the time, Congress also amended the Social Security Act to allow federal matching funds for state vendor payments for health care services for the elderly.

By 1956, the ground swell of support for NHI became noticeable, with special interest manifested in some kind of relief for the elderly. But the victory of Medicare and Medicaid in 1965 is most easily seen as the logical product of a unique decade.

185

The Day of the Underdog

"America will always go for the underdog in the long run, even if it created the underdog in the first place," observes Henrik Blum, M.D., emeritus professor at the University of California School of Public Health. During the mid-1960s, the underdog had its day.

John F. Kennedy, to a great degree, and Lyndon B. Johnson, to an unprecedented degree, believed in the federal government's right to involve itself in matters traditionally viewed as the business of the states. Furthermore, the national desire to make sense out of Kennedy's assassination strengthened Johnson's already formidable legislative hand. Johnsonian democracy, the growing pressure for health care enfranchisement of the vulnerable, and the accession of Rep. Wilbur Mills (D-AR) to chairmanship of the powerful House Ways and Means Committee made passage of Medicare and Medicaid only a matter of time.

Congress, meanwhile, had been sneaking into more health care enfranchisement anyway—by expanding matching funds for state health care programs for the elderly, extending health care benefits to military dependents, and approving state-federal funding of health care for the medically indigent. The final enabling event was passage of the Civil Rights Act of 1964, which permanently changed the relationship between the federal government and the states. By the time that Medicare was passed, almost everyone was in favor of the program's philosophy —if not its content—save for the American Medical Association, which inflicted significant political harm upon itself with its continued opposition.

The Economic Fruits Ripen

From 1966 to 1975, one of the greatest turnarounds began in what is normally (at best) a mercurial health care economy. First, the economic fruits of Medicaid and Medicare appeared. The medical cost component of the Consumer Price Index increased from 2.1 percent in 1965 to 6.5 percent in 1967. By then, Congress already was amending Medicaid to reduce cost overruns.

Hospitals were singled out for special attention from 1971 to 1974 during the Economic Stabilization Program. Congress also approved funding for HMOs as a means of controlling health care costs, as well as national health planning.

Illustration by Craig MacIntosh. Reprinted by permission of *The Minneapolis Star and Tribune.*

Despite the 1968 Republican victory, NHI proponents made their biggest congressional push in the early 1970s, culminating in the 1974 failure (by only one vote) of the Kennedy-Mills NHI proposal in the House Ways and Means Committee. After a battle lasting more than a quarter of a century, the massive escalation in health care costs would overwhelm the appeal of NHI after 1974.

Disenchantment Leads to DRGs

Of the three watershed factors in health care between 1976 and 1985, two had nothing to do with government health policy.

First was the recession of 1981–82 and its repercussions, including greater awareness among employers of health-benefits costs and greater awareness among state governments of Medicaid costs. That awareness was intensified by federal cutbacks in overall health care funding.

Second, the election of Ronald Reagan signaled a national disenchantment with government solutions for intractable problems; private-sector solutions to the health care cost dilemma became the order of the day. They worked, too, as private employers rushed in where government had feared, or had been unable, to tread.

Third, threats to the fiscal survival of Social Security and Medicare overwhelmed ideological niceties. In what many observers thought was the last gasp of federal cost-control efforts, Jimmy Carter's hospital cost-containment bill went down to congressional defeat twice in the late 1970s. But less than five years later, Congress enacted a Medicare prospective pricing system that set prices based on DRGS (diagnosis-related groups).

Prospective pricing is every bit as much of a government cost-control program, but because of the new system's use of market language and dynamics, it became politically acceptable. The question of whether government should intervene was settled in the 1960s; today, it is only a question of how.

Inspired by (and, in turn, inspiring) employer and payer activism, Medicare's new stance was that market economics—not government policy—should control the future of health care. The pendulum had swung again.

Policy Forged by Social Tensions

Many years ago, Mohandas K. Gandhi, when asked what he thought of western civilization, replied, "I think it would be a very good idea." One is tempted to say the same of U.S. health policy: We don't have one. Rather, the structure and financing of American health care is determined by the tensions within and among a series of opposing forces that alternate in dominance at any given time. These forces are:

● **Indecisiveness.** Our inability as a nation to determine whether we believe that health care is a market commodity, a social good, or both, depending on the situation. If a nation cannot make this basic determination, it is not surprising that health policy implemented in its absence tends to be quirky.

● **Fiscal ambivalence.** Although the U.S. public has declared—in its political expressions, in opinion polls, and by custom—that it believes health care is a right, it has shown a marked unwillingness to come up with the money necessary to make that statement operational. As a result, the United States and South Africa are alone among developed nations in not having formally declared access to health services as a right of citizenship.

- **Infighting.** This nation's love/hate relationship between its public and private sectors is probably more intense and more convoluted than in any other country. Again and again, government, which clearly holds responsibility for public health, has supported private providers while neglecting its own. Medicare and Medicaid were designed specifically to preserve freedom of choice of provider—a philosophical underpinning only recently undone by the cost-containment imperative—and over and over. Congress defeated government health-insurance schemes in favor of making private insurance more available through tax incentives and other means.
- **Quality vs. Cost.** The merry-go-round interrelationships among the cost of, quality of, access to, and effectiveness of health care is not a new phenomenon bred by the use of market incentives. Even a brief look at the legislation, studies, and reports of any decade in this century reveals that the pendulum of policy constantly swings toward spending to improve quality and access, and then toward controlling of the expenses thus engendered; toward efficiency and cost control, and then toward rectification of the inequities, maldistribution of care, and mortality and morbidity thus engendered. And it always swings back again.
- **Power shifts.** Who wields power in health care continues to bedevil all the parties involved, particularly those that do not hold power at the moment. At various times, dominant power has been in the hands of state and local governments, the federal government, physicians, providers in general, Congress, voters, insurers, and employers. Rarely is any of these interests without power; but the pattern is that a disproportionate amount of power is invested in the hands of one, then another, then another as we become disappointed by the performance of each in turn. Thus, the debate over competition versus regulation is, in fact, a false one; American health care has never been without either. The debate is really over who will be regulated, and who will benefit from competition.
- **Structure vs. financing.** As Professor Odin Anderson, of the University of Chicago and the University of Wisconsin, points out: The United States never came to grips with the fact that its health care *structure* developed almost entirely independent of its health care *financing.* The era of third-party payment—public and private—came well after the system's main elements were in

place. In fact, perhaps the only really new trend of the 1980s is the attempt to interrelate structure and financing—in the public sector (Medicaid and Medicare incentives to use HMOs and outpatient care), the provider sector (provider insurance and HMO formulations), and the private-payment sector (employers' and insurers' increasing role as providers, through HMOs or more directly). However, even here, predictions of revolution prove overenthusiastic.

Americans: Surprised by Results

Finally, in health care as in many things, Americans continue to be surprised by the logical results of their policy decisions. The legal definition of competence is the ability to understand and accept the consequences of one's own actions; yet a significant amount of American health care policymaking consists of efforts to cope with the effects of *previous* U.S. health care policies.

Medicare and Medicaid brought federal, state, and sometimes local governments into funding health care for some 50 million people. Yet when the programs proved expensive, everyone seems to have been taken unaware. When cost-based reimbursement fueled the enormous growth in hospital capacity, the intensity of health care, and the development of health technology, providers were blamed as though they somehow had reacted inappropriately. Medicare and Social Security alike simply did not take into account the fact that most of the 75 million people born between 1946 and 1964 eventually would grow old.

The Johnsonian programs of the 1960s doubled production of physicians from 7,574 medical school graduates in 1966 to 15,728 in 1983; but the first major statement that a physician oversupply might be in the works came in 1980.

And almost the entire policymaking structure is still resisting the idea that when public and private programs are cut back, that when hospital margins are narrowed, that when care of the poor is concentrated in a minority of institutions, the result is a massive increase in the number of medically indigent patients, and fiscal calamities for institutions that care for them.

Fifty Years of No Policy

The past 50 years of American health care nonpolicy have been marked by fits and starts, recurring tensions, reactions and

190

overreactions—a pendulum that ceaselessly swings from one extreme to the other, always leaving its mark, but also always retreating back to a more moderate position before it goes off in yet another direction to leave another mark.

There is talk once again of national health insurance, as the holes in private and public health care sponsorship become more apparent. Questions are being raised about quality. As the effectiveness and the distribution of health care once again come under scrutiny, voices are heard asking whether government needs to step in and moderate the excess of a private sector whose interests may not be in step with those of the population as a whole.

"Americans," Winston Churchill once remarked, "can always be counted on to do the right thing—once they have exhausted all the possible alternatives." In the search for either a national health policy or an acceptable substitute, many options remain unexplored. And despite the eccentric, sometimes frightening, and sometimes hilarious record of that search during the past 50 years, it is impossible to doubt the sincerity and commitment of those individuals engaged in the quest.

So who knows? Perhaps down one of those darkened pathways that still beckons, we will yet find the right thing to do.

RECOGNIZING AUTHOR'S POINT OF VIEW

This activity may be used as an individualized study guide for students in libraries and resource centers or as a discussion catalyst in small group and classroom discussions.

The capacity to recognize an author's point of view is an essential reading skill. Many readers do not make clear distinctions between descriptive articles that relate factual information and articles that express a point of view. Think about the readings in chapters four and five. Are these readings essentially descriptive articles that relate factual information or articles that attempt to persuade through editorial commentary and analysis?

Guidelines

1. The following are brief descriptions of sources that appeared in chapters four and five. Choose one of the following source descriptions that best defines each source in chapters four and five.

Source Descriptions

a. Essentially an article that relates factual information
b. Essentially an article that expresses editorial points of view
c. Both of the above
d. Neither of the above

Sources in Chapters Four and Five

———— Source Fifteen
"For-profit hospitals Making Health Care Worse" by Peter Downs.
———— Source Sixteen
"Investor-owned Hospitals Are Not the Problem" by John C. Bedrosian.

_____ Source Seventeen

"Medicare Should Be Privatized" by Peter J. Ferrara.

_____ Source Eighteen

"Government Commitment to Medicare Should Be Maintained" by the American Medical Association.

_____ Source Nineteen

"Overview of World Health Care Systems" by John L. McFarland.

_____ Source Twenty

"Health Care in a Communist Society" by the Government of the German Democratic Republic.

_____ Source Twenty-one

"Health Care in the Welfare State" by the Swedish Health Department.

_____ Source Twenty-two

"Health Care in the Free Market System" by the American Hospital Association.

2. Summarize the author's point of view in one to three sentences for each of the readings in chapters four and five.

3. After careful consideration, pick out one reading that you think is the most reliable source. Be prepared to explain the reasons for your choice in a general class discussion.

APPENDIX

Highlights from 50 Years of American Health Care

1936: A federal government report claims that 90 percent of Americans are receiving inadequate medical care.

1937: The Group Health Association HMO is founded in Washington, DC.

1938: The American Hospital Association develops a seal of approval for prepaid insurance plans; the seal is a blue cross.

Work begins on mass production of penicillin, discovered in 1928 by Alexander Fleming, M.D.

1939: Sen. Robert Wagner (D-NY) introduces a national health insurance bill, but like its many successors, it will not pass.

1942: The Kaiser Permanente HMO is founded.

1943: Congress adopts the Emergency Maternal and Infant Care Act to provide medical benefits for dependents of low-income servicemen.

1944: The Social Security Board's annual report recommends mandatory state health insurance.

1945: California Governor Earl Warren calls for mandatory state health insurance; the resulting bill is defeated.

1946: President Harry Truman announces his call for a program of compulsory national health insurance.

The Hospital Survey and Construction Act (the "Hill-Burton Act") passes.

1948: The Association of University Programs in Hospital Administration holds its first meeting.

1949: The Blue Cross Association is chartered in Illinois.

1950: In amendments to the Social Security Act, Congress approves provision of federal matching funds to states that subsidize health care for the elderly through vendor payments.

1952: The Joint Commission on Accreditation of Hospitals is established.

1954: Jonas Salk's vaccine against poliomyelitis is developed.

"Fifty years of U.S. Health Care Policy," *Hospitals.* Reprinted by permission from *Hospitals,* Vol. 60, No. 9, May 5, 1986. Copyright 1986, American Hospital Association.

1956: Federal health care benefits are extended to military dependents.

Congress expands support of state health benefits for the elderly.

The AFL-CIO endorses the idea of national health insurance.

1957: Rep. Wilbur Mills (D-AR) becomes chairman of the powerful House Ways and Means Committee.

Rep. Aimé Forand (D-RI) proposes federal funding of care for the elderly; his bill fails.

1958: The AHA officially acknowledges the possible need for federally supported health insurance for some populations.

1960: Hearings by the Senate Subcommittee on Problems of the Aged and Aging find wide support for health coverage for the elderly.

Congress passes the Kerr-Mills bill, providing joint federal-state assistance for the medically indigent.

The Eisenhower Administration presents a bill creating a "Medicare Program for the Aged" to Congress; although the legislation does not pass, the name sticks.

1961: The Task Force on Health and Social Security for the American People endorses health care benefits for the elderly through the Social Security program.

1963: Congress passes the Health Professions Educational Assistance Act, which provides federal funds to encourage training of various health professionals, including physicians.

1964: The Civil Rights Act of 1964 passes.

1965: The Social Security Amendments of 1965 (P.L. 89–97) are passed, creating the Medicare and Medicaid programs.

1966: Medicare and Medicaid become operational.

Congress passes the Comprehensive Health Planning and Public Health Service Amendments (P.L. 89-749).

Michael DeBakey, M.D., uses plastic arteries and a temporary artificial heart during cardiac valve replacement surgery.

The federal government declares that hospitals participating in Medicare are subject to the provisions of the Civil Rights Act.

1967: The medical care component of the Consumer Price Index, which totaled 2.1 percent in 1965 and 2.9 percent in 1966, jumps to 6.5 percent.

Christiaan Barnard, M.D., conducts the first human heart transplant operation.

1968: Walter Reuther, director of the United Auto Workers, announces that he will form a "Committee of 100" to press for comprehensive national health insurance.

1969: The Department of Health, Education, and Welfare Task Force on Medicaid and Related Programs is created.

1970: The Health Security Act, a national health insurance plan, is introduced in Congress; it and many others like it will fail in the 1970s.

1971: The Economic Stabilization Program is inaugurated.

1972: Congress passes the Social Security Amendments of 1972, which create the Professional Standards Review Organization program, fund dialysis and transplants for victims of end-stage renal disease, and give the federal government more cost-containment authority.

1973: The Health Maintenance Act is passed, greatly increasing federal financial support for HMOs.

1974: Economic Stabilization Program controls end.

The Kennedy-Mills bill dies in a House committee, ending the high point for national health insurance.

Hawaii passes the Prepaid Health Care Act, thus becoming the first (and still the only) state to mandate employer-provided health insurance for all employees.

1975: The National Health Planning and Resources Development Act is passed.

A New Jersey court allows Karen Ann Quinlan's parents to withdraw life support from their permanently comatose daughter.

1977: President Jimmy Carter proposes the Hospital Cost Containment Act.

The AHA and fellow organizations launch the Voluntary Effort to Contain Health Care Costs.

1978: Carter's hospital cost-containment legislation fails in Congress.

In Great Britain, the first baby conceived outside the human womb is born.

1979: Carter's hospital cost-containment bill fails again.

The Carter Administration submits a national health insurance bill to Congress; it doesn't pass either.

1980: Per capita U.S. health care expenditures reach $1,075, an increase of more than 300 percent since 1970.

The Graduate Medical Education National Advisory Committee issues a report predicting an oversupply of U.S. physicians by the 1990s.

New Jersey institutes a prospective pricing system that uses DRGs.

1981: Congress passes the Omnibus Budget Reconciliation Act.

The worst recession since the 1930s hits the United States.

The AHA, the AMA, the Blue Cross and Blue Shield Association, the AFL-CIO, the Business Roundtable, and the Health Insurance Association of America endorse private-sector initiatives to control health care costs.

1982: Congress passes the Tax Equity and Fiscal Responsibility Act.

1983: Congress passes legislation establishing Medicare's DRG-based prospective pricing system.

1984: Per capita U.S. health care expenditures reach $1,632, an increase of more than 50 percent since 1980.

BIBLIOGRAPHY

Aday, Lu Ann, Ronald Anderson, and Gretchen V. Fleming. *Health Care in the U.S.: Equitable for Whom?* Beverly Hills, Calif.: Sage Publications, 1980.

Davis, Karen. "Access to Health Care in a Cost-Conscious Society." In *Access to Health Care: Who Shall Decide What?*, edited by Helen Rehr. Lexington, Mass.: Ginn Press, 1986.

Davis, Karen. "Health and the Great Society: Revisited After Twenty Years." *Lyndon B. Johnson Library Symposium, The Great Society: A 20 Year Critique,* April 18–19, 1985.

Davis, Karen, Marsha Gold, and Diane Makuc. "Access to Health Care for the Poor: Does the Gap Remain?" *Annual Review of Public Health* 2(1981): p. 51.

Dutton, Diana. "Explaining the Low Use of Health Services by the Poor: Costs, Attitudes or Delivery Systems?" *American Sociological Review* 43 (June, 1978): pp. 348–68.

Kravits, Joanna. "The Relationship of Attitudes to Discretionary Physician and Dentist Use by Race and Income." In Anderson, et al. *Equity in Health Services:* pp. 73–93.

Lerner, Monroe, "Social Differences in Physical Health." In *Poverty and Health: A Sociological Analysis.* Cambridge: Harvard University Press, 1975.

McKinlay, John B. "The Help-Seeking Behavior of the Poor." In *Poverty and Health: A Sociological Analysis,* edited by John Kane and Irving Kenneth Zola. Cambridge, Mass.: Harvard University Press, 1975.

MINORITIES
Blacks

Cooper, R., et al. "A Note on the Biologic Concept of Race and its Application in Epidemiologic Research." *American Heart Journal* 108(1984): pp. 715–23.

Cooper R., et al. "Prevalence of Diabetes/Hyperglycemia and Associated Cardiovascular Risk Factors in Blacks and Whites: Chicago Heart Association Detection Project in Industry." *American Heart Journal* 108(1984): pp. 827–33.

Easterling, R. E. "Racial Factors in the Incidence and Causation of End-Stage Renal Disease." *Trans. of the American Society for Artificial Internal Organs* 23 (1977): pp. 28–33.

Eckenfels, E. J., et al. "Endemic Hypertension In a Poor, Black, Rural Community: Can It Be Controlled?" *Journal of Chronic Diseases* 43(1977): pp. 499–518.

James, S. A. "Socioeconomic Influences on Coronary Heart Disease in Black Populations." *American Heart Journal* 108(1984): pp. 669–72.

Langford, H. G. "Is Blood Pressure Different in Black People?" *Postgraduate Medical Journal* 57(1981): pp. 749–54.

National Urban League. "The State of Black America, 1985." Washington, D.C.: January 1985.

Rice M. F., and W. Joans. "Black Health Inequities and the American Health Care System." *Health Policy and Education* 3(1982): pp. 195–214.

Williams, P. B. "Assessing Awareness of Coronary Disease Risk Factors in the Black Community." *Urban Health* 8(1979): pp. 34–37.

Hispanics

Ailinger, R. L. "Hypertension Knowledge in a Hispanic Community." *Nursing Research* 3(1982): pp. 207–210.

Anderson, R., et al. "Access to Medical Care Among the Hispanic Population of the Southwestern United States." *Journal of Health and Social Behavior* 22(March, 1981): pp. 78–89.

Bornstein, F. P. "Gallbladder Carcinoma in the Mexican Population of the Southwestern U.S." *Pathology and Microbiology* 35:189–191, 1970.

Braucht, G. N.; Loya, F.; and Jamieson, K. J. "Victims of Violent Death." *Psychological Bulletin* 3:300–327, 1980.

Castro, F. G., et al. "Risk Factors for Coronary Heart Disease in Hispanic Populations: A Review." *Hispanic Journal of Psychology* (1985).

Center of Health Statistics. California Cohort Study Preliminary Data. State of California, Dept. of Health Statistics, August 1984.

Davis, C.; Haub, C.; and Willette, J. "U.S. Hispanics: Changing the Face of America," *Population Bulletin* 38(3) Population Reference Bureau, Inc., Washington, D.C., 1983.

Lowenstein, F. W. "Review of the Nutritional Status of Spanish Americans Based on Published and Unpublished Reports Between 1968 and 1978." *World Review of Nutrition and Dietetics* 37:1–37, 1981.

Lyndon B. Johnson School of Public Affairs. *The Health of Mexican-Americans in South Texas*. Policy Research Project. Report No. 32. 1979.

Menck, H. R. "Cancer Incidence in the Mexican American. *National Cancer Institute Monograph* 47:103–106, 1977.

National Center for Health Statistics. Trevino, F. M., and Moss, A. J. Health Indicators for Hispanic, Black, and White Americans. *Vital and Health Statistics.* Series 10, No. 148. DHHS Pub. No. (PHS) 84–1576. Public Health Service. Washington, D.C.: Supt. of Docs., U.S. Govt. Print. Off., 1984a.

National Center for Health Statistics. Ventura, S. J. Births of Hispanic Parentage, 1981. *Monthly Vital Statistics Report.* Vol. 33, No. 8 Supp. DHHS Pub. No. (PHS) 85–1120. Hyattsville, Md.: Public Health Service, 1984b.

National Center for Health Statistics. Ventura, S. J. Births of Hispanic Parentage, 1980. *Monthly Vital Statistics Report.* Vol. 33, No. 6 Supp. DHHS Pub. No. (PHS) 1–18. Hyattsville, Md.: Public Health Service, 1983.

Proceedings of the Conference on Maternal and Child Health Along the Mexico/U.S. Border. El Paso, Texas, Nov. 13–14, 1981.

Selby, M. L.; Lee, E. S.; Tuttle, D. M.; et al. "Validity of the Spanish Surname Infant Mortality Rate as a Health Status Indicator for the Mexican-American Population." *American Journal of Public Health* 74:998–1002, 1984.

Stern, M. P.; Gaskill, S. P.; and Allen, C. R., Jr. "Cardiovascular Risk Factors in Mexican-Americans in Laredo, Texas. II. Prevalence and Control of Hypertension." *American Journal of Epidemiology* 113:556–562, 1981b.

Stern, M. P. "Does Obesity Explain Excess Prevalence of Diabetes Among Mexican-Americans? Results of the San Antonio Heart Study." *Diabetologia* 24(1983): pp. 272–77.

Trevino, F. M. and A. J. Moss. "Health Indicators for Hispanic, Black, and White Americans." *Vital and Health Statistics* 10(148, 1984). DHHS Pub. No. (PHS) 84–1576. Public Health Service, Washington, D.C.; Superintendent of Documents, U.S. Government Printing Office.

Weisfield, V. Robert Wood Johnson Foundation *Special Report.* 1:3–11, 1983.

Indians

American Hospital Association. *American Hospital Association Guide to the Health Care Field,* 1984 edition (Chicago, IL: AHA, 1984).

American Indian Health Care Association. *The Urban Indian Health Program* (St. Paul, MN: American Indian Health Care Association, no date).

Beiser, M., and Attneave, C. L. "Mental Disorders Among Native American Children: Rates and Risk Periods for Entering Treatment." *Am. J. Psychiatry* 139(2):193–198, Feb. 1982.

Berman, A. *An Analysis of Suicidal and Non-Natural Deaths Among the Duck Valley Reservation Indians* (Washington, DC: American University Press, 1979).

Charleston, G. M., Myers, J. G., and Charleston, K. *Indian Alcoholism Program Evaluation Fiscal Year 1984* (Oklahoma City, OK: Datastat Computer Center, 1985).

Deloria, V. "The Popularity of Being Indian: A New Trend in Contemporary Indian Society." *Centerboard: The Journal of the Center for Human Relations Studies* 2(1):6–2, Spring 1984.

"Dental Care in American Indian and Alaska Native Children." *Morbidity and Morality Weekly Report* 34(26):400–401, July 5, 1985.

Fischler, R. S. "Child Abuse and Neglect in American Indians." *Child Abuse and Neglect* 9(1):95–106, October 1983.

Gibson, R. M., and Waldo, D. R. "National Health Expenditures, 1981." *Health Care Financing Review* 4(1):1–35, September 1982.

Herman, D. J. "Oral Disease Prevention/Oral Health Promotion." *The IHS Primary Care Provider* 9(12):1–4, December 1984.

Klausner, S. Z., and Foulks, E. F. *Eskimo Capitalists: Oil, Politics and Alcohol* (Totowa, NJ: Allanheld, Osmun, 1982).

Macro Systems, Inc. "Indian Health Service, Contract Health Services, Final Report," prepared for the Office of the Assistant Secretary for Planning and Evaluation, U.S. Department of Health and Human Services, Washington, DC, March 1984.

Macro Systems, Inc. "Final Report of an Assessment of Private Insurance Coverage and Medicare/Medicaid Reimbursement Among Indians Eligible for Health Care Provided by the Indian Health Service," prepared for the Office of the Assistant Secretary for Planning and Evaluation, U.S. Department of Health and Human Services, Washington, DC, June 1984.

Mail, P. D. "American Indian Alcoholism: What Is Not Being Done?" *The IHS Primary Care Provider* 9(3):1–5, March 1984.

May, P. A., and Hymbaugh, K. J. "A Pilot Project on Fetal Alcohol Syndrome Among American Indians." *Listening Post: A Periodical of the Mental Health Programs Indian Health Service* 5(3):3–16, October 1985.

National Diabetes Advisory Board. *The Prevention and Treatment of Five Complications of Diabetes* (Atlanta, GA: 1983).

National Indian Health Board. "IHS Slated for $10.8 Million Cut in '86 Under Gramm-Rudman." *NIHB Health Reporter* 4(20):1–4, January 1986.

National Tribal Chairmen's Association, testimony before hearing of U.S. Congress, House of Representatives, House Committee on Interior and

Insular Affairs, H.R. 1426, Indian Health Care Improvement Act of 1985, Washington, DC, Mar. 19, 1985.

Prucha, F. P. *Americanizing the American Indian* (Cambridge, MA: Harvard University Press, 1973).

Shore, J. H. "American Indian Suicide—Fact and Fantasy." *Psychiatry* 38:86–91, Feb. 1975.

Sievers, M. L. "Hypertension in Native Americans." *The IHS Primary Care Provider* 9(7):6–7, July 1984.

TCI, Inc. "Indian Self-Determination Study," prepared for the Bureau of Indian Affairs, Assistant Secretary of the Interior, Indian Affairs, Washington, DC, May 1984.

U.S. Department of Health and Human Services, Public Health Service, National Center for Health Statistics, *Health, United States, 1984,* DHHS Pub. No. (PHS) 85–1232 (Washington, DC: U.S. Government Printing Office, December 1984).

Westermeyer, J. "Erosion of Indian Mental Health in Cities." *Minnesota Medicine* 59(6), June 1976.

Wilson, M. "The Federal Trust Responsibility and Obligation to Provide Health Care to Indian People." Research Institute on Legal Assistance of the Legal Services Corp., internal document, Mar. 10, 1980.

Young, J. L., Ries, L. G., and Pollack, E. S. "Cancer Patient Survival Among Ethnic Groups in the United States." *Journal of the National Cancer Institute* 73(2):341–352, August 1984.

RA
418.5
.P6
P66
1988

RA
418.5
.P6
P66

1988

13.95